The Patriarchal Paradox

The Patriarchal Paradox

Women Politicians in Turkey

Yeşim Arat

Rutherford ● Madison ● Teaneck
Fairleigh Dickinson University Press
London and Toronto: Associated University Presses

Associated University Presses
440 Forsgate Drive
Cranbury, NJ 08512

Associated University Presses
25 Sicilian Avenue
London WC1A 2QH, England

Associated University Presses
P.O. Box 488, Port Credit
Mississauga, Ontario
Canada L5G 4M2

The paper used in this publication meets the requirements
of the American National Standard for Permanence of Paper
for Printed Library Materials Z39.48-1984.

Library of Congress Cataloging-in-Publication Data

Arat, Yeşim, 1955–
    The patriarchal paradox: women politicians in Turkey / Yeşim
Arat.
        p.   cm.
    Revision of thesis (Ph.D.)—Princeton.
    Bibliography: p.
    Includes index.
    ISBN 0-8386-3347-1 (alk. paper)
    1. Women in politics—Turkey. 2. Patriarchy—Turkey. 3. Turkey—
Politics and government—1960–   I. Title.
HQ1236.5.T9A73   1898
320′.088042—dc 19   88-45715
                                                                          CIP

Printed in the United States of America

To my Mother and my Father

Contents

Preface

The question as to why there are so few women in politics prompted this work. However, the study as it is addresses the issue through a series of other questions that explore how women, in contrast to men, move from the private to the political realm. Who are these few women who have broken the male political monopoly? By virtue of which capacity were they able to do so? Was their entry into politics spurred by the intention of representing women? Or was the pursuit of power itself a goal that attracted them? Did these women, in trying to enter politics, confront a hostile male political edifice; or were men indifferent to, or perhaps supportive of, female political aspirations?

These questions have been considered significant enough to deserve much attention.[1] While the feminist debate continues as to whether or not women should exercise power in politics in the way men do,[2] empirical studies that shed light on women politicians abound. This work explores such questions in the context of women politicians in Turkey.[3] Precisely because of the paucity of their numbers and the unique context in which they assumed political office, these women might, in any case, have had a claim to our attention. By penetrating a monopoly of male power they were, after all, pioneers in an important democratic endeavor. These were, moreover, Muslim women expressing themselves in a political medium that was both secular and democratic, yet within a context in which the legacy of neither secular nor democratic politics was firmly embedded. Over a short period of time, Turkish society had emerged from an Islamic authoritarian background as a secular westernizing state.

What is perhaps more striking about Turkish women is that during the process of transition, they did not have to organize themselves into a protest movement or a pressure group to struggle for their political rights. The founding fathers of the Turkish Republic, under the leadership of President Kemal Atatürk, granted full rights of citizenship to women about a decade after the War of Independence (1919–23). A series of reforms that culminated in the granting of universal women's suffrage by 1934 improved women's legal status in society. Men rather than women promoted women's rights in Turkey. This legal and political equality—quite unusual at the time, both because there was no women's movement pressuring for these rights and also because many Western democracies did not then allow women a comparable status—provided the macro framework in which women could move from the private to the political realm.

To pursue questions on women in Turkish politics and gather data beyond published material, I conducted a series of in-depth interviews over a period of six months in 1981 with a group of politicians: sixteen female and ten male members of the Parliament, and twelve female members of municipality councils.[4] Even though my focus was on women parliamentarians, some male members of the Parliament as well as female municipality council members were interviewed for comparative purposes.

Intensive interviewing was particularly useful in bringing into focus the thoughts and feelings of the politicians themselves. As the political actors themselves shape the issue of political office holding to some extent, what they say on the subject and how they say it needs to be taken seriously. Studying the transcribed interviews gives us the opportunity to probe deeply into these politicians' worlds and try to understand "the ways in which they interpret their own actions and the actions of others."[5] Throughout my interviews the respondents had the opportunity to explain themselves at length, defending their responses, at times contradicting what they said and thereby revealing the complexities of their thoughts and actions. Thus I could seek to develop explanatory propositions regarding women politicians in Turkey.

The introduction of this book explicates the framework in which the study is located. The first two chapters present an overview of the Turkish context where women in Turkish politics belong. The chapters that follow introduce the politicians interviewed and raise questions on their initiation into politics, their career lines, and the obstacles they confront.

Acknowledgments

This project began as a Ph.D. dissertation at Princeton. John Waterbury guided me through the enterprise, promptly reading and acutely criticizing my work. I would like to thank him very much. I am deeply indebted to Suzanne Keller. Her challenging suggestions, perspicacious criticism, and generous encouragement made it possible for me to give shape to my research. Bernard Lewis recognized my interests before I did, helped me choose my topic, and directed me accordingly. Charles Issawi liberally extended his help and advice whenever I needed it. I would also like to acknowledge my gratitude to two of my undergraduate teachers at Yale, Charles Lindblom and David Levine, who cultivated my respect for the social sciences and shaped my thinking.

Many friends also helped and encouraged me at different stages of the project. Among them, I would like to mention Beenu Mahmood, Sabri Sayarı, Diane Sunar, and Nur Altınyıldız. At a critical turning point, Mary Fainsod Katzenstein offered her generous suggestions and encouraged me to publish the manuscript. Uday Mehta's special friendship, invaluable criticisms, and support sustained me all along. Finally, I would like to acknowledge my husband, Şevket Pamuk, who patiently helped me revise and complete the manuscript for publication.

Clearly, this work would not have been possible without the Turkish politicians I interviewed. Their cooperation was crucial and they made the interviewing exciting for me. I thank them very much.

1

Introduction: Patriarchy and Women in Politics

Why is the issue of women's public life and political office holding significant enough to be studied? The response to the question is controversial in the context of feminist debate. The controversy revolves around the question of how women should exercise power in politics. Two opposing arguments prevail.[1] One is presented by those who espouse an equality based on general human rights. Accordingly, if women are to be equal to men, then they should strive for every possible power base men have. Whatever the value of women's norms or values in the private realm, women are ultimately dependent on men who hold power in the public realm.[2] Politics, as the realm of the contingent where human beings can take collective action to determine their common fate, is a particularly important arena. Hence, if women are to be equal to men, then they should participate equally in political decision making concerning their common public lives.

The alternative view is presented by those who claim that women are "separate but equal" to men.[3] This view upholds the differences between men and women. Accordingly, the woman's sphere of the private realm can be a source of strength and identity (for women) as opposed to the man's sphere of the public realm.[4] Opportunities for domestic influence, religious morality, and child nurture in the woman's realm can allow women to exercise a social power based on their special female qualities. In other words, the argument is made that women exercise their power differently from men.

Among those who seek a recognition of women's separate identities and sources of strength, at times the claim is made that women need not compete for political power in the way men do. In her acrimonious language, Barbara Watson makes the argument that "for women to move into the power structure is a capitulation to masculine values and one that involves . . . complicity with a (man-made) destructive social order."[5] Hence participating in traditionally recognized political institutions is not merely unnecessary, but also detrimental to women's norms. Women should create the realm of politics that is most congenial to their concerns rather than collaborate with men in a political undertaking where the rules of the game are written by men.

Within the context of these two seemingly contradictory feminist perspectives lies the significance of women's marginality in assuming political office. If our ultimate goal is to promote women's "separate as well as equal" status—that is, to acknowledge women's difference from as well as equality to men—it might not be enough merely to take a separatist stand. Important as it is to work outside the established power structure, it is also necessary to gain power from within. Popular recognition of women's separate realms needs to be translated into legislative endorsement before considerations of equality can be meaningful. The alternative is acquiescing to unequal status. Within representative institutions, women can introduce a woman's perspective over a broad range of issues. They can bring in their experiences as daughters, sisters, wives, or mothers to contribute in traditional women's fields such as educational and family policies. Women can advocate new life-styles based on an acknowledgment of their "separate but equal" status. The failure to secure institutional recognition of women's differences will alienate women from the polity that they intend to change. If there are too few women in politics to initiate change on their own, the question as to why there are not more comes up. On the other hand, if women in politics, regardless of their numbers, do not or cannot bring about change, we still need to discern the reason.

If, on the other hand, we act on the assumption of general human rights rather than the "difference principle" it follows that male/female equality involves the participation of women in political decision making. The question of why there are so few women in politics is duly appropriate. To find out why, further questions about the socio-economic backgrounds, career lines, and recruitment patterns of the male and female politicians need to be answered: the issue of women's problems in politics has to be explored.

How do we explore the issue? Different theoretical approaches are possible. The two commonly used approaches are the "political socialization" and the "structural" approach. The political socialization approach emphasizes the role of childhood learning to explain gender differences in political disposition and by implication in political representation.[6] Accordingly, girls are encouraged to develop domestic concerns while boys learn to be interested in public matters and eventually assume the political tasks in society. The political socialization thesis as such tends to verify rather than explain the existence of a sex-differentiated culture with its particular socialization processes. A critical assessment of the reasons underlying sex-differentiated socialization is left undone. More specifically, the significance of the social structure where political socialization takes place is ignored.

The structural approach offers an alternative to the political socialization thesis in explaining gender differences in political participation. Under the rubric of the structural approach, some explanations trace the cause of women's lower level of participation to specific structures such as "role structures" or "opportunity structures," which have limited functions within society.[7] Others, on the other hand, question the fundamental organization of the structure of the society, assuming the root of the problem to be the structure of the entire social system that is the economic structure of the society, capitalist or socialist, or the social structure of the society, patriarchal or communal. These explanations draw attention to the logic of the whole social structure and focus on the broader question of women's lower status within the society rather than merely their lower level of political participation. Marxist explanations, which focus on the economic structure of society,[8] and patriarchal explanations, which focus on the male-female power dynamics, are such examples.

In this book, I shall underline the patriarchal structuring of our polity to throw light on the systemic causes of women's apolitical roles. The patriarchal approach has been developed by feminist authors such as Simone de Beauvoir, Viole Klein, Kate Millet, Shulamith Firestone, and Zillah Eisenstein in the twentieth century.[9] Despite significant differences in perspective, they make the same basic argument. Patriarchy they say, is a structure of power that endorses male supremacy. Society is organized around this patriarchal principle whereby women are subordinate to men. The family, the society, the economy, and the polity are interrelated patriarchal units in which "the relationship between the sexes is one of dominance and subordinance".[10] Within this system, they conclude, women are disadvantaged in regards to participating in politics. In other words, the asymmetrical power relations between men and women help to explain women's socially inferior status and lower level of political participation.

Patriarchal explanations focus on a power relation that exists at different levels of society. It is generally agreed that this relationship originates in the act of giving birth.[11] A convincing explanation as to how reproduction shapes patriarchy is that the woman who bears children is also expected to rear them.[12] Although for the woman, giving birth might be a biological mandate, raising the children is a dictate of social conduct. Within this arrangement, women become dependent upon men as men have access to the public realm to earn the family's living. The patriarchal relationship that evolves within the context of the family results in men holding economic power in society and wielding authoritative power within the polity. The patriarchal ideology generated by the underlying patriarchal structure helps to perpetuate this system of male supremacy through the mass media and through religious and educational, as well as economic and political institutions.

Patriarchy is thus seen as a structure of domination that is legitimate. Domination in the Weberian sense of power is "the possibility of imposing one's will upon the behaviour of other persons."[13] To the extent that every form of domination needs self-justification, the tradition of male authority helps to justify and legitimize patriarchy. Consequently, patriarchal power is not necessarily based on force but rather on authority. The authoritative power wielder has the "right to command" because of shared norms.

The concept of patriarchy as feminist theorists use it overlaps with the Weberian conception to the extent that tradition is a source of legitimation in both cases. This overlap, however, is clearly limited, if not incidental. According to feminists, tradition by itself is not the only means of legitimation. Men occupy powerful positions in the economic and the political realm and assume the legitimacy that such positions entail. A woman obeys the husband who is the breadwinner or the brother who is more educated and informed about public matters. To the extent that those who occupy powerful socioeconomic positions can shape the lives of men and women in society and the society consents to this order, these positions have a legitimacy. Laws and customs reinforce this legitimacy. The press and religion and language in school or within the family serve both to perpetuate male rule and also to legitimize it.[14] Feminist theorists view patriarchy as a general structure of domination with different bases of legitimation. In viewing patriarchy as a general structure of domination, they dispense with Weber's specific use of the term, which tends to limit the applicability of this concept to personal loyalty legitimized through tradition.

Defined as a structure of domination, patriarchy is a fixed power relationship. This definition recognizes power as a form of subjugation exerted by one group over another, resulting, in Michel Foucault's words, in "a system whose effects through successive derivations pervade the entire social body."[15] Accordingly, the male-female relationship in which men dominate women is reflected within the "entire social body," the state as well as the economy, the family as well as the school. Within this framework, the power of the subjugator is emphasized while the power of the subjugated is underplayed. It is implicitly assumed that women have a submissive, passive role within the patriarchal relationship. In other words, the "power of the weak" is ignored. The possibility of women's revolt (to male dominance) or women's separate realms of power do not become serious issues.

Yet in a patriachal relationship where men dominate, women nevertheless generate their own power that this particular feminist conceptualization overlooks. The power of the weak is best recognized if power is defined as a shared and ongoing process rather than a fixed structure of domination. Power must be understood, Foucault argues "as the moving substrate of force relations which by virtue of their inequality, constantly engender states of power, but the latter are always local and unstable."[16] Accordingly, unproportional male power activates women's power. This conceptualization might be better suited to study the power of the weak, namely women in a relationship of domination. When we assess patriarchal theory as feminist theorists endorse it, we need to underline its overarching focus: patriarchy defined as a structure of power that endorses male supremacy focuses on male power at the cost of overlooking women's power. As a theoretical tool, it highlights best the implications of men's power or authority as it shapes or influences women's. Nevertheless, within the parameters of a patriarchal society as feminists define it, male rule might well be dominant and this particular approach seeks to probe into its nature.

With its focus on power dynamics between genders, the patriarchal explanation can throw light on sex-differentiated political socialization. Because of their traditional access to the public realm, men occupy positions of power women do not. In turn, men in the public realm become role models for boys who are then socialized to adopt those roles that traditionally bestow patriarchal power on men. Girls, on the other hand, learn to play their future domestic roles that screen them from public authority and recognition. To the extent that men have power at different levels of society and that women are unaware of its patriarchal nature, women can not or do not challenge the traditional division of labor between the sexes in the private and the public realms. The sex-differentiated political socialization is perpetuated.

The patriarchal approach is similar to the Marxist explanation in that both offer a structural explanation of politics. In both cases, there is an attempt to study the underlying social organization of the society in order to diagnose the fundamental structures generating gender differences. However, unlike the Marxist explanation, the patriarchal approach highlights the central importance of gender relations. The unequal power relation between men and women, although shaped by the economic structure of the society, is not merely derivative of that structure. Access to the public realm is at the heart of the patriarchal relationship regardless of the particular economic structure that defines this public realm. Economic power, although a crucial element in substaining patriarchy, cannot provide an exhaustive account of its dynamics or legitimacy.

In this book, women in Turkish politics are examined within the framework of a patriarchal explanation. It is assumed that dynamics of male-female power relations need to be explored above and beyond considerations of social class. Patriarchy is understood to be an asymetrical power relation between men and women that endorses male supremacy. The definition is a broad one intended to reflect the different manifestations of the patriarchal reality that shape different aspects of our social life, rather than concentrating on one particular patriarchal occurrence. With this broad definition, the way the prevailing patriarchal organization of society affects women in politics is explored.

Despite the unique circumstances that set the Turkish case apart from many others, Turkish women nevertheless had to move to the political realm in a patriarchal society. As such, they shared many similarities with women of different cultures. As in other patriarchal societies, men were more educated, economically more powerful, and politically more autonomous than women. In the context of a society where men have more power than women, it is assumed that the unequal power relation between men and women works against women to keep them away from politics (as well as other realms). Because women do not have the socio-economic and political resources men do, many obstacles make it difficult for them to enter politics and compete effectively with men.

Studies on women politicians support the argument that male power can be a hindrance for women who want to assume political office.[17] Women politicians consider male cliques and biases to be a formidable problem at different stages of their political careers. Women complain that they do not have equal access to the resources men do. Men can acquire the necessary funds, establish the right contacts, cultivate the patronage links and, in so doing, be more credible candidates for political office than women can be.

Only when male power is subordinated to women's do women seem to succeed in politics. Women who have beat the many odds against them and have been successfully active in political life, for example, often have had atypically activist mothers.[18] In a typical patriarchal relationship, mothers are subordinate to the fathers (in familial decision making or financial control). Yet, in the case of successful women politicians or activists, mothers who have not been dominated by their husbands seem to be the norm. These dominant mothers, in many ways, serve as role models for their daughters who come to succeed in political life.[19]

The Turkish case, however, was different. Within the prevailing patriarchal structure, the skewed structure of power between men and women was precisely what prompted women to participate in politics, as well as kept them away from it. Male support was crucial for women politicians. As previously mentioned, men who founded the Turkish Republic promoted women's rights. In other words, at the macro level, the founding fathers of the republic provided the framework in which women could participate in politics. At the micro level, fathers and husbands influenced and encouraged women to participate in politics; male politicians recruited them. Yet once in politics, there were limits to male support.

What was the precise nature of male support? To what extent were women politicians conscious of male power in politics? In the context of a patriarchal society, what were the particular circumstances conducive to women's initiation into politics? What, if any, were the obstacles to political success under these circumstances? This work raises such questions to probe into the nature of the power dynamics between men and women to shed light on women politicians' careers in Turkey.

The responses to these questions will be given in a context in which it is assumed that patriarchy as a structure of power manifests itself in different forms within the historically specific context of particular societies. Turkey, with her secular Kemalist ideology, has to come to grips with an Islamic-Ottoman legacy. The patriarchal approach is well suited to analyze the dilemmas of Turkish society to the extent that it provides a matrix whereby women's problems with their Islamic and Kemalist dimensions can be studied in terms of power relationships. Neither Islam nor Kemalism as ideologies or ways of life are mere reflections of the patriarchal nature of the Turkish society. Nevertheless, a close interaction exists between them. Islam, as well as Kemalist ideology, have not only introduced and legitimized, but, at the same time, promoted and perpetuated patriarchal ways of life.

2
Patriarchy in Turkish Society

In 1927, four years after the proclamation of the Turkish Republic, there were rumors that the Women's Association (Kadınlar Birliği) of the day would nominate women candidates in the coming elections. When reporters asked Nakiye Elgün, a prominent leader in the War of Independence, who later became one of the first women members of Parliament, what she thought on the issue, she answered,

> Why don't we nominate some women candidates? Because the law does not permit it. Therefore it is not our time yet. Our government has granted us every right our women deserved, in fact more than deserved.[1]

Elgün's remark is revealing not merely because it shows us how the patriarchal norms inhibit even the most political of women, but also because it points to the critical role men (and their patriarchal power) played in promoting women's rights. Like a typical Turkish woman, Elgün had internalized the patriarchal system to such an extent that going beyond its laws was unthinkable. She expected the male ruling elite to initiate any change that they deemed appropriate. In this chapter, I shall trace the changing nature of Turkish patriarchy with which the Turkish women have to grapple.[2] To the extent that women were passive in demanding these changes, men had their own reasons for initiating change. Today, women still contend with the opportunities and constraints of a patriarchal society that men were crucial in shaping. "Man-made" reforms could increase women's access to the public realm, but retain the obstacles that prevent equality or liberation for women.

Ottoman Patriarchy

THE LEGAL STATUS OF WOMEN

The nineteenth and early twentieth centuries were periods of rapid social change.[3] However, until the turn of this century, the legal

status of women in urban Ottoman society was mainly defined by
the Sharia Law of the Hanefi School, at times supplemented by the
law (kanun) of the sultan. These kanuns were based on the Sharia,
which they could supplement but not contradict. The Sharia
assumed that women were naturally dependent on men, which
meant that because they were not men's equal, they needed the
protection of men.[4] Laws regulating marriage and family life
allowed polygamy; a man was legally entitled to four wives as long
as he could support them and treat them all fairly.[5] Men also had the
exclusive right to dissolve their marriages. The institution of one-
sided divorce by men (talak) allowed the husband to repudiate his
wife even when she had not breached the marriage contract.[6] He
need only provide alimony (nafaka) to the divorced wife.[7] It was not
until 1917 that the Law of Family Rights introduced rules and reg-
ulations ameliorating the conditions of married women. Marriages
contracted without the recognition of the state were henceforth un-
lawful. The law made it obligatory for a man wanting to marry a
second wife to gain the permission of the first. In cases of adultery
(zina), women were not qualified to bear witness; four male wit-
nesses were to provide evidence.[8]

Concubinage was commonly recognized by Islamic law. Female
slaves, captured in war or bought in slave markets, were employed
in households—usually as domestic servants, and sometimes as wet
nurses, singers or dancers.[9] Men and women could own slaves of
either sex; furthermore, a man was legally entitled to cohabit with
his female slaves. Imperial decrees prohibiting the slave trade were
issued in 1854 for white slaves, and in 1857 for black slaves.[10] Abolition was more stringently enforced after Turkey's participation in
the 1890 Act of the Brussels Conference.[11] By the early twentieth
century few slaves were left.

Ottoman women could own property; however, inheritance laws
recognized male relatives' right to a larger share of inherited property, usually twice the portion of the female.[12] The Tanzimat Land
Reforms in the second half of the nineteenth century allowed
daughters to inherit land on terms similar to those of male heirs.[13]

Finally, what needs to be emphasized in regard to the legal status
of Ottoman women is the issue of seclusion. Despite some mitiga-
tion of conditions in the late nineteenth and early twentieth centuries (as will be discussed in more detail), women were secluded
from men, especially in the higher classes.[14] In public, women were
expected to wear veils and to cover themselves.[15] Very few were employed in public sectors, although this situation was changing to
some extent. In the homes of the upper and middle classes, as well
as in the sultan's palace, women lived in separate quarters called the

"harem," the word revealingly derived from "haram," meaning that which is forbidden.[16] As these examples suggest, women were by law both subordinate to men and confined to a private and separate realm.

THE SOCIO-ECONOMIC STATUS OF WOMEN

Within the boundaries defined by law, some women did exercise considerable authority. Marriage, and especially maternity, sanctified by religious statements (such as "Heaven is under the feet of the mother") and upheld by custom, secured a certain recognition for women. In the sultan's harem, the women who bore the sultan's children were raised to a higher status within the harem.[17] A somewhat similar situation prevailed among the ruling elite in general. What the English letter-writer Lady Mary Montagu in the eighteenth century observed with amazement regarding matrimony was still true in the nineteenth century among upper middle classes. She wrote:

> Any woman that dies unmarried is looked upon to die in a state of reprobation. To confirm this belief they reason that the end of the creation of women is to increase and multiply; and she is only properly employed in the works of her calling when she is bringing up children, or taking care of them, which are all the virtues that God expects from her. And indeed their way of life, which shuts them out of all public commerce does not permit them any other.[18]

Giving birth was an auspicious occasion, deserving special celebration.[19] The mother, in addition, had substantial influence over her children. It was the mother who arranged the choice of spouses when her children came of age.

The women of the upper classes, including those of the sultan's harem, did indeed lead a life of leisure. As the English traveller Lucy Garnett described it, they spent their time "paying calls, attending weddings (düğüns), promenading, driving, shopping and going to the baths."[20] Having maids, cooks, and slave girls, they could absolve themselves even of household duties. Those who had the means, especially the women of the sultan's harem, established pious foundations such as wakfs and subsidized mosques and institutions of higher learning (medreses). For example, the Pertevniyal mosque, completed in 1871, was donated by the wife of Sultan Mahmud II.[21] However, upper class women, by and large, were a leisure class. The nineteenth century Ottoman intellectual Namık Kemal's criticism of these women is revealing:

Women, especially in the last thirty years, have withdrawn from participating in activities completely, becoming solely companions of pleasure like musical instruments and jewelry. Except for propagating, they contribute nothing else to mankind.[22]

Women in the lower and middle classes who did not have the funds or leisure developed domestic skills and managed their houses. Lucy Garnett wrote of these women:

[They] having so few interests outside the home are naturally very domesticated and no accomplishments are so much appreciated in the average marriageable maiden as the domestic arts of working, laundry and needlework. Much time is also devoted to embroidering the scarves, towels, sheets, quilts and other articles destined to figure in the trousseau of a Turkish girl.[23]

The aspirations of these classes were largely restricted to tending their homes.

EDUCATION

Women's lack of education reinforced their confinement to domestic roles. In Ottoman society, educational opportunities were limited for boys as well as for girls, but particularly for girls.

Apart from private tutoring, the only education offered before the nineteenth century was religious education in privately-funded primary schools (subyan mektepleri). In these schools, boys and girls were taught religious lessons, elementary arithmetic, and simple reading and writing.[24] Higher education in the medreses was reserved for boys.

After nineteenth century reforms, educational opportunities for girls, although continuing to lag behind those for boys, did improve significantly.[25] In 1858, the first junior high school (rüşdiye) for girls was opened. Until 1911, when the first senior high school (idadi) opened, higher education was provided by the Girls Teachers College, founded in 1870.[26] In 1914, the University for Girls, affiliated with the Girls Teachers College, was established.[27] The few technical schools, notably those in Üsküdar and Yedikule, provided training in sewing, embroidery, and cooking skills. In conformity with the norms of seclusion, female teachers and, at times, old male teachers taught in the girls' schools.[28]

Besides public education, private training in the arts was available for girls from upper class families. Those who could afford private tutors learned foreign languages, drawing, painting, and the piano. The educational institutions of society protected the Ottoman patriarchy in which men and women had separate worlds. The question was how long this separation would continue.

"Indoors was the delicate, intimate rule of women, out of doors was the realm of men." So the Turkish feminist Halide Edip Adıvar described the division of labor in early twentieth century Ottoman society.[29] However, confronted with economic pressures, the impact of the West, and the demands of conscription (especially during the 1912–13 Balkan War), women began moving out of the "intimate indoors" into the realm of men.

Traditionally, lower-class women, mainly slaves, had been employed by the rich as domestic servants. Increasingly, women of free birth took such jobs.[30] Besides domestic labor, they worked at various jobs from street sweeping to industry. More than 50 percent of those employed in the textile industry, especially in cotton and silk-thread production, in the late nineteenth and early twentieth century were women.[31] In 1897, women constituted half of the workers in the Istanbul Match Factory.[32] During World War I, middle class women replaced conscripted men in post offices and the civil service.[33]

Women had always been midwives, treating gynecological disorders, and teachers, instructing women in the Quran, poetry, and music. In these roles within the private realm, they did not challenge the system of seclusion. Gradually, however, they were employed as nurses and secondary school teachers in hospitals and schools.[34] Women even began trading grain and food products in the streets of Istanbul.[35]

Not all the women who stepped out of doors and into the public realm were employed in the workforce. Many came out of their harems and households to provide social services. The Red Crescent Women's Center, the Navy Association Women's Branch, Art House, and the Society of Guardianship were social organizations formed around 1912 to provide services to immigrants and the widows of soldiers, and to teach them such crafts as sewing or embroidery.[36] These seemingly insignificant developments led to major shifts in the organization of an entire way of life. Rigid boundaries between the male and female realms were becoming perforated.

WOMEN'S RIGHTS

This influx of women into the public realm was accompanied by a debate over women's rights. Paradoxically, men rather than women initiated the debate. Leading intellectuals of different disciples questioned and criticized the prevailing status of women through novels, conferences, and philosophical treatises. Although most proponents of change agreed that women needed to be educated, those views were invariably constrained by the ideal of enlightened mothers and good wives. Namık Kemal's argument in "A Draft on Education of Women" states:

> In our land, women are totally ignorant and unaware of their rights and responsibilities advantages and detriments . . Hence the ignorance and illiteracy of our women of course leads their children in similar directions while their natural proclivities for love and affection which have not been restrained by right or wrong usually leads them to spoil their children in every way.[37]

Perhaps the most influential intellectual to elaborate on the meaning of emancipation was the Turkist leader Ziya Gökalp. Gökalp, the theoretical architect of Turkish nationalism, emphasized three aspects of the women's issue: women's participation in socio-economic life, equal education as men, and equal treatment under the law.[38]

While such arguments provoked heated responses, mainly from Islamists, women advocates soon participated in the debate as well. They began writing in magazines and newspapers published by or for them on subjects ranging from the vices of polygamy to the virtues of child care. *Terakki* (Progress), published in 1868, *Hanımlara Mahsus Gazete* (Newspaper for Woman), published in 1895, *Mahasin* (Magazine) and *Kadın* (Woman) published in 1908, were examples of such papers and journals.[39] Among the women who wrote on women's issues in the late nineteeth and early twentieth centuries, Fatıma Aliye was clearly the most prominent. Her response to the Islamist Mahmud Esad's defense of polygamy is a celebrated polemic against that institution. Women could no longer be contained within their separate world. The code that prescribed such a separation was being questioned.

Transition to Republican Patriarchy

WAR OF INDEPENDENCE

The status of Ottoman women was further upgraded during the War of Independence. The war (1919–23) precipitated effective role changes, both because women had to assume men's jobs after men were recruited for the army, and also because they fought alongside men in battle.

In urban areas, many women earned their living in industries that manufactured clothing for the army.[40] During the occupation of Istanbul, they organized public protest meetings to mobilize men and women against the occupying forces. Women speakers such as Halide Edip Adıvar, Nakiye Elgün, and Münevver Saime incited crowds to patriotism at Sultanahmet, Fatih, Üsküdar, and Kadıköy meetings, important demonstrations that testified to women's newly emerging public voice.[41]

In Sivas, Anatolia the Anatolian Women's Association for Patriotic Defense was established. Its active members, mainly wives and daughters of men in the Kemalist cadres, supported the national war by organizing meetings, writing protest letters to the wives of leaders of the occupying forces, and, at times, raising funds.[42] Even though there is little published material to throw light on the extent of the organization's activities, it is known that branches were established in other Anatolian towns, namely Amasya, Kayseri, Niğde, Erzincan, Burdur, Konya, and Kastamonu.[43]

In the field, some women fought alongside men. Soldiers and commanders in the War relate women's deeds of bravery.[44] The case of Nezahat Hanım, named Joan of Arc of the Turks by some soldiers, is documented in parliamentary records because the Parliament considered granting the War of Independence medal to her.[45] The Statue of the War of Independence in Ulus, Ankara, which portrays a Turkish woman carrying ammunition alongside an armed man, pays homage to the women who fought in the war.

KEMAL ATATÜRK AND WOMEN'S RIGHTS

Even though the War of Independence proved that women could successfully assume so-called men's tasks, it did not radically alter entrenched customs and roles. Women who fought for their country and earned their living did not demand the legitimacy, let alone the extension, of their newly-acquired roles. As leaders and founders of republican Turkey, men set the stage for the granting of social as well as political rights to women in the 1920s and early 1930s. The reforms introduced by men secured a legal status for women far in advance of their actual position in Turkish society at that time. However, the reforms were the grounds which made concrete improvements possible. Şerif Mardin aptly argues that the Turkish Revolution was "primarily a revolution of values" where "innovations, such as . . . the reform in the status of women were directed at changing prevailing values." Improvements in women's status were both a means to change traditional values as well as an end in themselves.

In 1926, the Turkish Civil Code, modeled after the Swiss Civil Code, was adopted. This code improved the social status of women by abolishing polygamy, endorsing compulsory civil marriage, recognizing the right of divorce for both partners, and accepting egalitarian inheritance laws. In 1930, changes in the municipality law gave women the right to elect members and to be elected to the municipality councils. Finally, in 1934, the male members of the fourth Parliament recognized the right of women to elect members and to be elected to the National Assembly. Besides these specific reforms, the process of secularization that abolished the caliphate in 1924, undermining the religious establishment, prepared the ground upon which reforms could be effective.[47] As religious institutions had recognized and reinforced a patriarchal society, their dissolution signified the loss of a source of legitimacy for patriarchy. The patriarchal society that could no longer appeal to religion as source of its justification changed its form and became milder, even if it did not wither away.

Even though it is indisputable that major reforms in the status of women were initiated and implemented by Kemal Atatürk, many questions remain on this issue. The legal equality accorded by these reforms was quite progressive, especially when one considers that even many Western democracies did not then allow women a comparable status. For example, women in France and Switzerland did not receive the right to vote until 1944 and 1960, respectively. In view of such considerations, one is liable to view the Turkish reforms as anomalous historical accidents. Why did Atatürk introduce these reforms? Was the granting of women's rights an important issue for its own sake or was it a strategic move to serve other ends? What was the significance of the timing of the reforms? Why was the right of women to sit in the Parliament not recognized at the time the staunchly pro-Atatürk Parliament passed the legislation on their right to be elected to municipality councils?

Several explanations throw light on these questions. Afet İnan, a Western-educated Turkish woman whose education Atatürk personally supervised, and Tezer Taşkıran, a professor of philosophy, member of Parliament, and the daughter of a leading liberal intellectual of the Kemalist era, both emphasize Atatürk's personal interest in women's rights as an issue that needed to be promoted for its own sake. Afet İnan explains how Atatürk respected women as mothers and patriots.[48] Women needed and deserved to be educated. Taşkıran argues that to promote women's rights without opposition, Atatürk introduced the reform bills one by one, according to "a carefully planned strategy which recognized rights equal to those of men first in the family, then in the local community and finally in the governing of the state."[49] She suggests that reform bills were an end in themselves and that their piecemeal introduction was a tactical move to ensure acceptance without opposition.

Dankwart Rustow[50] and Lord Kinross[51] focus on the psychological dimensions of the issue. In their attempts to explain the emancipation of Turkish women, they underline the importance of Atatürk's personality. Both try to draw a link between Kemal the man and Kemal the political leader and dwell on his personal relations with women. The implication is that had Kemal had a different relationship with his mother or his wife the unfolding of the women's reforms might have taken a different turn.

An alternative view is presented by Şirin Tekeli. Tekeli argues that the reform bills on women's rights were means to an end rather than ends in themselves. "When the reforms were introduced," she argues, "the main goal was not securing women's active political participation per se, but rather, utilizing the symbolic value of women's entry to the parliament."[52] She further argues that when charges were made against Atatürk insinuating that he was another Hitler establishing a nationalist, one-party regime, women's enfranchisement was a means to distinguish Turkey from the Nazi Germany of "Küche, Kinder, Kirche" and prove to the Western world the democratic nature of the Turkish Republic.[53] Tekeli further claims that legislation on women's political rights passed in two stages (1930 and 1934) because the leadership wanted to draw attention to the country's commitment to democracy one more time. Otherwise, she claims, the second Parliament, which voted on women's right to participate in municipality elections, was ready at the time to vote on any legislation supported by Atatürk, including women's right to participate in the parliamentary elections.[54]

Even though Atatürk regarded the issue as significant in itself, the recognition of women's political rights should also be considered as a means to an end, as Tekeli argues. However, the issue needs to be discussed in a broader context: the enfranchisement of women was part of an attempt to improve women's status, which, in turn, was a means of westernizing, not merely democratizing, the country. The westernization, defined by Atatürk as the process of belonging to the ranks of civilized countries, required the establishment of a secular, national, as well as democratic, state.[55] Unless women had equal status not only in the social, but also in the political realm, the state could not be fully democratic, secular, or even truly national.

To make a persuasive argument that the improvement of women's status including enfranchisement was dictated by the desire to westernize, one needs to discuss the intellectual tradition from which Atatürk emerged. From Ziya Gökalp to Abdullah Cevdet, reformist Ottoman intellectuals who nurtured Atatürk's political ideas, believed in improving the status of women.[56] Judging from Atatürk's own comments on the issue, the improvement of women's status was conceived as a dictate of the secular, national and democratic state, namely the western republic that Atatürk intended to establish.

The question of women's rights was one of secularization. While religious conservatives opposed the improvement of women's status, Western observers maintained that Islam was the cause of women's subjugation.[57] From the late nineteenth century on, even before the question of the franchise for women was raised, Islamists strongly objected to changes of women's status in aspects of marriage, divorce and polygamy.[58] The improvement of women's status thus meant undermining the legitimacy of the Islamists as well as deflecting Western criticism. In a speech he gave at İzmir in 1923, Atatürk revealed a sensitivity on the question of Islam, women, and Westerners:

> Our enemies accuse us of being prisoners of religion and attribute our decline and degradation to it. This is a mistake. Our religion never decreed women to be lower than men. God decreed that Muslims, men and women, pursue knowledge together.[59]

As early as 1923, he was disturbed by the charges of Westerners, concerning Islam and women, who did not accept the Muslim Turks. Although he tried to justify the improvement of women's status in Islamic terms, Atatürk was troubled by the charges of Westerners. Both religious opposition and western criticism on this issue of Islam and women's status needed to be settled. Giving full rights of citizenship to women, after the change in family laws, was a final blow to the religious opposition who had already lost the caliphate, the fez (Islamic headgear), and the Arabic script. At the same time, such a move was a gesture to the West to show that Muslim women were not subjugated by Islamic law in secular Turkey. Republican Turkey was now ready to be accepted by the civilized West.

Similarly, recognizing women's rights was a means of asserting the national character of republican Turkey. The Turkish state, unlike the Ottoman Empire, was based on the Turkish nation. In Mustafa Kemal's words, "The Turkish Revolution mean[t] replacing an age-old political unity based on religion with one based on another tie, that of nationality."[60]

In view of revisionist Turkish history, the national traditions of the Turks dictated that men be equal to women. The claim was made that according to pre-Islamic Turkish custom, women participated equally in public life. Even though Mustafa Kemal rejected the utopic visions of a pan-Turkish state, he was much influenced by the Turkish intellectuals who argued for the primacy of the national bonds and the high status of women according to national traditions:[61]

> In our nation, in historic times women really possessed the highest status.[62]

> Studying Turkish history, one sees that in Turkish social life women have never been lower in status in knowledge, culture or other respects (than men).[63]

These passages are from Atatürk's speeches in which he hails the Turkish woman and shows her to be integral to Turkish history. In Ottoman times, the Turkish women of Anatolia worked and cooperated with men, unlike the Ottoman women of Istanbul.[64] However, misperception prevailed: foreigners, namely Westerners, who observed subjugated Ottoman women mistakenly thought of Ottoman as Turkish ways. Thus, Atatürk argues:

> The women described and depicted by foreigners and those who see us as enemies are not the real women of this country, that is the real Turkish women of Anatolia. Such women [that is, the ones they depict] do not exist in the real life of the real country. Those who misperceive and mistake Turkish women, are deceived by the appearance of some Turkish ladies in those places that are mistaken to be civilized especially in our large cities. . . . They [the foreigners] attribute the characteristic they observe in these women who are few and limited in numbers to all the Turkish women. This is the first fault that needs remedy and the first truth that will be proclaimed. You all know and it is well known that one meets the women they describe in Istanbul, the largest city of our country which has been the capital of the state and the caliphate for hundreds of years.[65]

In loyalty to the Turkish heritage, the subjugated Ottoman woman should be replaced by the Turkish woman with equal rights and responsibilities to the man. Such a move was a means of asserting the Turkish nationality of the new republic, and a way, to preempt premature Western criticism. Turkey would thus become a nation-state reflecting its liberal national traditions as did other Western nation states.

Finally, democracy prescribed the promotion of women's social and political rights. As Afet İnan relates, Atatürk posed the issue of women's rights as a question of democracy. In a discussion with statesmen and intellectuals where all agreed that women's political rights must be recognized, Atatürk concluded:

> A Republican regime means governing of the state with a democratic system. We founded the Republic; as it reaches its tenth year, all the dictates of democracy need to be fulfilled one at a time. Recognition of women's rights is such a necessity. Be assured.[66]

Women's rights were a dictate of the secular, national, and democratic republic Mustafa Kemal intended to establish. Only thus could the formal criteria of inclusion in the ranks of Western nations be met. Although more research needs to be done on the circumstances that led up to women's enfranchisement, the process might have been completed in two stages because of consideration of public opinion.

Before many Western countries, Turkey recognized full rights of citizenship for women. This crucial event prompted by the exigencies of westernization perhaps preempted the emergence of a women's movement such as those found in Western countries. Such a movement might have heightened women's consciousness of being underprivileged in the public realm. Leaving aside these conjectures and putting the historical facts into perspective, Turkish women's social and political rights were man-made privileges that served the grand design of westernization. Men, rather than women, insisted on recognizing women's rights to westernize the country. Turkey did become a westernizing state that was secular, national, and aspiring to democracy. Turkish women, at least in the urban areas, began to assimilate this national ethos.

The Kemalist reforms undeniably improved the status of women, loosening the bonds of the private realm and opening the doors to the public realm. But could Turkish women stride through, now that they had formal access? Would the emulated Western standards be sufficient to put women on a par with men? Did not Western women have their own problems not deserving of emulation? What was the nature of these problems? Such were the questions that were not asked by the founding fathers of the republic when they prepared the public arena for their daughters to enter.

Republican Patriarchy

LEGAL FRAMEWORK

The new civil laws, which radically improved the legal status of women in society, nevertheless have their patriarchal biases.

According to the Turkish Civil Code, the husband is formally the representative of the marriage union (Civil Code, clause 154).[67] The husband decides the place of residence of the married couple (Civil Code, clause 152). Unless she has the husband's permission to do otherwise, the wife must adopt the husband's surname. In cases of divorce, the ultimate decision concerning guardianship over children is again the husband's. The wife who wants to earn her living needs the husband's permission, though there are restrictions to keep the husband from exercising this right arbitrarily (Civil Code, clause 159).[68]

Other seemingly egalitarian laws work against women within the context of the society. The law recognizes separate personal ownership of property between spouses. This law ignores the fact that most married women are housewives, taking care of the family at home, while their husbands earn the money to acquire personal property.[69] Women's work at home subsidizes the purchase of the husband's property during their married life. Neither divorce nor inheritance laws recognize the housewife's unaccounted contribution of labor towards the husband's property.

EDUCATION

Since the foundation of the republic in 1923, the number of educated women increased considerably in Turkey. According to 1975 statistics, the number of women with elementary school degrees in the 20–29 age group (1,257,569) was about ten times that of those in the 50–59 age group (125,808). At the high school level for the same groups, the increase was ninefold (from 9,500 to 85,805). The number of women with university degrees in the 20–29 age category was seven times more than that in the 50–59 age category.[70]

The increase in absolute numbers was not paralleled by an increase in the proportion of women among the total number of graduates. The percentage of women among those who were illiterate increased from 73 percent in the 50–59 age group to 80 percent in the 20–29 age group.[71] The younger generation which had a larger proportion of illiterate women as compared to the older generation had proportionately fewer women among secondary school graduates (27 percent of the total graduates are women in the 20–29 age category against 31 percent in the 50–59 age category). At the elementary school level, the percentage of women among total graduates increased by 7 percent in the 20–29 age group in relation to the 50–59 age group (36 percent of the total graduates are women in the 20–29 age group against 29 percent in the 50–59 age group). Only at the university level was there a substantial increase in the percentage of women graduates: in the 20–29 age group, the percentage of women among university graduates was 26 percent, twice that of the 50–59 age group. Table 1 shows the percentage of women and men according to age group and last school graduated.

Table 1
Gender Breakdown in Different Age Groups According to Last School Graduated (1975)

Last School Graduated	Age Groups							
	20–29		30–39		40–49		50–59	
	women	men	women	men	women	men	women	men
Elementary School	36	64	34	66	28	72	29	71
Secondary School	27	73	30	70	34	66	31	69
Lycee	27	73	25	75	26	74	27	73
Higher Education	26	74	23	77	14	86	13	87
Illiterate	80	20	77	23	70	30	73	27

With 50 percent of the female population illiterate, Turkey has a high female illiteracy rate not—only higher than Western countries such as Italy, France, or the United States, but also higher than Middle Eastern countries such as Jordan and Kuwait.[72] On the other hand, the percentage of females in primary, secondary and higher-level Turkish schools tends to compare favorably with many Middle Eastern countries, although they are lower than Western countries.[73]

An important aspect of the gender differences in Turkish education that the above statistics do not reveal is the significance the place of residence has on sex differentials in education. In Turkey, gender differentials are noticeably larger in rural areas. Table 2 shows the urban/rural differences in female to male education according to 1970 census data.[74]

Table 2
Female to Male Ratios in Schools According to Place of Residence (1970)

	Urban	Rural
Primary School	6:10	4:10
Secondary School	5:10	2:10
High School	5:10	2:10
Higher Education	3:10	10:10

The figures indicate the number of female graduates for every ten male graduates at different levels of education. While males are always more educated than females, whether in rural or urban residence, sex differentials are higher in rural areas than urban areas except at the higher education level. Opportunities for higher education are very limited for males as well as females. Hence, having the means and motivation to get a university degree are factors that seem to override gender differences in access. For every male in a rural residence who has a higher education, there is a female with similar qualifications.[75] However, as the Turkish proverb runs, "oğlunu seven hocaya, kızını seven kocaya verir" (the one who likes his son gives him away to a teacher, the one who likes his daughter gives her away to a husband).

ECONOMY

Although education is not the single determinant of labor force participation, men who, as we have seen, are better educated than women, participate in the labor market as wage earners more than do women. According to the 1975 census results, 64 percent of the total population above the age of 12 who are economically active are men and 36 percent are women.[76] Statistics on economic activity by age group show that male/female ratios in the labor force have not changed significantly over the years.[77]

Table 3
Gender Breakdown of the Labor Force in
Different Age Groups (1975)

Age Group	Women	Men
25–29	32	68
30–34	33	67
35–39	36	64
40–44	34	66
45–49	33	67
50–54	36	64
55–59	37	63

Among the women in the labor force, a large majority (about 90 percent) has been and still are in the agricultural sector.[78] Table 4 indicates the sectoral distribution of the female labor force between 1955 and 1975.[79]

Table 4
Sectoral Distribution of Female Labor Force (1955–1975)
Percent of Total Female Labor Force

Sector	1955	1960	1965	1970	1975
Agriculture	95.6	95.0	94.1	89.0	89.9
Industry	2.3	2.7	1.5	5.1	3.5
Services	1.6	1.9	2.6	5.0	7.4
Other	0.5	0.4	1.8	0.9	0.2

Outside the agriculture sector, especially in the industrial sector, male/female segregation is striking. While 50 percent of the people in agriculture, forestry, hunting, and fishing are women (mostly unpaid family workers), only 5.9 percent of the population in electricity, gas, and water, 4.4 percent in transport and communication, and 11 percent in community, social, and personal services are women. In finance, insurance, real estate, and business services, women make up 23 percent of the total, and, in manufacturing, 20 percent.[80]

If we look at the data on women's economic participation from the perspective of the occupations they have rather than the industries in which they are employed, we still find a pattern of segregation. As in Western countries only a small percentage, 1 percent, of the managers, directors and top-level administrators in Turkey are women. Women engaged in trade make up about 3.3 percent of the population in the field. Meanwhile, nursing and secretarial work are predominantly women's occupations. There are no male students in either nursing or secretarial schools.[81]

Within this picture of a segregated labor force, Turkey has a high percentage of female professionals. According to 1975 statistics, women scientific and technical workers and professionals make up 27 percent of the total.[82] Although this high percentage includes figures for nursing as well as teaching, two rather typical female professions, law and medicine, are a significant percentage, even compared with women in most other occupations and women lawyers and doctors in Western countries.

Before discussing why this is the case, it is appropriate to document the issue further. On the basis of the Union of Bar Association's statistics and government statistics for medical school diplomas, Ayşe Öncü calculated that 19 percent of lawyers and 15 percent of the physicians in Turkey are women.[83] In the urban Istanbul area, the proportion of lawyers reached as high as 28.5 percent in 1978. According to 1972 U.S. Bureau of Census data, the percentage of women lawyers and judges in the United States was 3.8.[84] The proportion rose to 9.4 percent in 1978. In West Germany, only 7.5 percent of state attorneys (based on 1973 figures) were women.[85] According to the *Handbook of International Data on Women* (1970 figures), Turkey had more female law graduates than such Middle Eastern countries as Lebanon and Egypt as well as many Western countries, including Italy, the United Kingdom, West Germany, and the United States.[86]

In medicine, Turkey compared favorably with Western countries in its number of female doctors. About 15 percent of Turkish doctors in 1970 were women, whereas the figure was 11.3 percent for the United States as late as 1978.[87] In West Germany, according to 1978 figures, 15 percent of specialist physicians were women.[88] Compared to Eastern bloc countries where female doctors make up half of those in the profession, the significance of the Turkish figures clearly diminishes.[89] However, the Turkish figures are, nonetheless, striking in the Turkish as well as in the Western context.

Why are there relatively so many women lawyers and doctors in Turkey? It is argued that the growth of these prestigious professions is relatively new. Under conditions of rapid expansion, especially in the absence of entrenched sex-linked stereotypes, the elite status of these professions is maintained by the admission of upper and middle class women.[90] Because of large class inequalities, upper class women can employ lower class women for household help; otherwise, the extended family network can be relied on to relieve the professional woman.[91] This argument leads us to expect that there be more women in other newly expanding professions such as engineering, which in fact is not the case. It ignores the fact that women doctors and lawyers can be self-employed and need not integrate into larger male-dominated institutions. Both of these professions allow women to have potentially large female clienteles. Furthermore, it might also be noted that as there were always some women doctors or midwives, that fact might have further enhanced women's interest in medicine. Nevertheless, this argument does throw light on the conditions under which so many women become lawyers and doctors.

Besides lawyers and doctors, a high percentage of teachers in Turkey are women. However, even though there are many women in teaching as compared to other occupations, teaching is less of a female profession in Turkey than it is in Western countries. At the elementary school level, according to 1970 and 1977 statistics, 34 percent and 41 percent, respectively, of teachers in Turkey were women.[92] The corresponding figures for the U.S. between 1972 and 1978 were 85 and 84 percent, more than double the Turkish figures. Likewise, in Germany in 1979, 63 percent of elementary school teachers were female. At the secondary school level, Turkish figures ranged between 32 and 37 percent (1970–78). In the United States, the figures were around 50 percent (1972–78).[93] In Germany they ranged between 35 percent in high schools to 52 percent in technical high schools.[94] In Turkey, 23 percent of the teaching staff in higher education were women in 1979.[95] In the United States, in 1975, the figure was 28 percent.[96]

Looking over the data on Turkish women's economic status it can be said that even when Turkey compared favorably with other countries, women did not have the economic status men did. The proverb, "girl at home, boy at work," held true. Now I shall look at the status of women compared to men in the family.

FAMILY: THE POWER STRUCTURE

Studies based on large-scale surveys in Turkey show that the patriarchal joint family, where families of different generations live together, has been largely replaced by the nuclear family.[97] About 60 percent of all families are nuclear, as opposed to 20 percent that are joint patriarchal.[98] Urbanization, industrialization, and the emerging system of property and production relations have altered the family structure.[99]

However, although the family structure has changed, the conjugal power structure in the family seems to remain patriarchal, that is, the male authority, at least formally, persists. Family power structure is difficult to operationalize and study empirically.[100] There is no consensus among social scientists as to what resources—such as education, income, and occupation—shape the dynamics of conjugal power structure, even though it is agreed that these factors do alter the familial power relation.[101] Even a duofocal family structure in which "the husband and wife have a clear differentiation of tasks and a considerable number of separate interests and activities" might not alter the hierarchal organization of power within the family.[102] It is doubtful that a non-hierarchical power balance can be maintained within a family where the wife has limited access to the public realm, and has insignificant economic and political power. Although women do exercise authority in their separate realms, this does not necessarily mean that they can maintain a non-hierarchical power balance within the family, especially when they are not the breadwinners.

Case studies carried out in Turkey indicate that industrialization and urbanization affect conjugal role relations, enabling the wife to participate more fully in important familial decisions.[103] Other studies show that although resources such as education or occupation are important in changing the conjugal power relation, the wife's resources determine the balance of power in her favor more than the husband's resources do in his.[104] There is a direct relationship between the professional and familial status of women. According to Çiğdem Kâğıtçıbaşı's research, women's status in the family defined in terms of "mutual decision making, role sharing and communication between men and women" increases as her professional status does. A professional or an administrator has the highest status in the family, while the agricultural worker has the lowest.[105]

Despite evidence of the increasing power of women under changing circumstances, fathers and husbands nevertheless retain formal authority in the family. According to Serim Timur's study of the Turkish family structure conducted with a nationwide sample of 4,500 households, men and women alike perceived husbands or fathers to "have more say," that is, more authority, in family matters than wives or mothers did.[106] Even though the nationwide sample does not reflect differences in authority structures according to income, occupation or place of residence, it shows overall trends according to different family types. Tables 5 and 6 summarize the results of the survey.[107]

As the tables indicate, 74.2 percent of men and 62.0 percent of women in all families agree that it is the husband who has more say in the family. The percentages are much higher if we consider that 18.4 percent of the males and 17.5 percent of the females say that the husband's father, not the husband—still a patriarchal head— has the most say in the family. In nuclear families the percentages are still higher: 94.3 percent of the men and 88.8 percent of the wives think that the husbands have the most say in the family. Regardless of family type, "the one with the most say" is always a male patriarchal figure.

When the question is who decides on expenditure of the family income, the answers are no less clear. Men and women claim that in about 72 percent of the nuclear families the husband decides; in 31.5 percent of the patriarchal joint families, the husband is again the one who decides, while in 59.8 percent it is the elders. Overall, 58.1 percent of the husbands and 20.2 percent of the elders decide on the expenditure of the family income. Only in 15.6 percent of all the families do the spouses decide together. The number of women who decide on their own is negligible.[108]

Çiğdem Kâğıtçıbaşı, who uses a nationwide sample in a study on

Table 5
According to Family Type, Who Has More Say
in the Family: Male Responses

| Who has more say | Family type | | | | |
	Nuclear from start	Nuclear later	Transient Joint	Patriarchal Joint	All Families
Male (himself)	94.3	95.2	75.2	28.2	74.2
Wife	1.2	0.8	0.6	0.4	0.7
Husband's father	0.1	2.0	8.6	61.5	18.4
Husband's mother	0.7	0.4	10.1	4.1	2.9
Wife's mother or father	0.0	0.0	3.1	0.4	0.5
Other	3.6	1.6	2.4	4.4	3.3
Total %	100	100	100	100	100

Table 6
According to Family Type, Who Has More Say
in the Family: Female Responses

| Who has more say | Family type | | | | |
	Nuclear from start	Nuclear later	Transient Joint	Patriarchal Joint	All Families
Husband	88.8	85.7	55.9	17.2	62.0
Woman (herself)	3.2	4.5	2.9	1.9	3.2
Husband's father	0.6	2.5	6.7	53.9	17.5
Husband's mother	0.2	0.6	19.0	13.5	7.1
Woman's parents	0.0	0.2	7.9	0.0	1.4
Other	8.2	6.5	9.6	13.5	8.8
Total %	100	100	100	100	100

the value of children in Turkish society, finds similar responses to questions on authority relations within the family. A total of 78 percent of those in the sample, men and women, say that "mostly the husband" decides on buying something expensive.[109] Regarding the number of children the family should have, 56 percent say it is the husband and 11 percent say it is the wife who decides.[110] At least formally, men are the authoritative partners in marriage.

POLITICS

Male authority prevails in politics as well. Women defer to the authority of their male relatives when they have to make political choices. Social scientists document the apolitical character of Turkish women from various perspectives. Frederick Frey, on the basis of his survey of Turkish villages, concludes that in rural areas where women traditionally participate in the rural economy as agricultural workers, "political dimension constitute[s] an important distinguishing component of the male role."[111] Even when women participate in the labor force, as they do in the rural areas, they do not necessarily develop political interests.

Beşir Atalay, in his study of an Anatolian village near Ankara, documents that among 40 women and 70 men who answered his questionnaire, 85 percent of the women (34 women) and 24.5 percent of the men (17 men) said they were not interested in politics at all, while 74 percent of the men (52 men) and 5 percent of the women (2 women) said they were intereested in politics.[112] One of the women who expressed political interest said she was interested in politics because of the influence of her parents, relatives, or husband.[113] Among married women about 80 percent (15 out of 19) said they supported the party their husband supported. Among the unmarried, 90 percent of the girls (24 out of 27) as opposed to 47 percent of the boys (33 out of 57) said they supported the same party as their father.[114]

Oya Tokgöz, in her research on political communication and women carried out in Çankaya, an urban Ankara district, showed how women know less about politics than men; even the mass media is not particularly effective in promoting their political involvement.[115] For example, in her survey of 497 people, 20.8 percent of the women as opposed to only 1.2 percent of the men could not identify any of the political parties. Of the men, 36.9 percent, as opposed to 9.7 percent of the women, could identify all of the political parties participating in an election.[116] In the same survey, 8.2 percent of the women as opposed to 24.2 percent of the men said they were "very interested" in political news prior to elections. Thirty percent of the women and 14.6 percent of the men said they were not interested in political news at all.[117]

In a different survey conducted again in urban Ankara, Ahmet Taner Kışlalı shows that not only are women less interested in politics than men, but that women rely on their husbands to form their political beliefs.[118] Of the women who responded to Kışlalı's questionnaire, 32.7 percent said that their spouses shaped their political choices. None of the men gave that answer. The number of women who said that they made their political choices themselves (54.4 percent of the women) was almost half the number of men who decided on their own (93 percent of the men).[119] Politics was a male realm.

PATRIARCHAL VALUES IN THE SOCIETY

Common proverbs and sayings reveal the authoritative position of men in the society from an alternative perspective. Most of the proverbs refer to men as "er," which literally translates as warrior/soldier, with connotations of the brave, the fighter or the soldier.[120]

With a few exceptions, all maxims celebrate men as the strong, the valiant and the breadwinner.[121] Men are valued: as the saying goes, "Oğlan doğuran övünsün, kız doğuran dövünsün" (Let the one who bears a son be proud, let the one who bears a daughter beat herself). Men are strong: "Er düştüğü yerden kalkar" (The one who is a man rises when he falls). Men persevere: "Er olana gayret gerek" (Stamina is what suits the one who is a man). Men have authority: "Er başından devlet ırag olmaz" (Prosperity is not afar from men). Men are breadwinners: "Er olan ekmeğini taştan çıkarır" (The one who is a man digs his bread from stone).

Popular proverbs tell us that women are subordinate, domestic figures ordained to marry and depend on men. Women are intellectually inferior: "Kadının bildiğini garip de bilir" (Even the nitwit knows what the women knows); "Kadının saçı uzun aklı kısadır" (Women's hair is long, brain is short). Women's place is at home: "Kız evde, oğlan işte" (Girl at home, boy at work); "Kız evde tanınır oğlan tezgahta" (One recognizes the girl at home, the boy on the work-table). Women's place is in the kitchen with the children: "Kadıneli kaşık sapından kararır" (The hand of a woman is blackened from the handle of a spoon—that is, from cooking and feeding children). Women's vocation is to marry and have children: "Kızı duvak, gelini beşik arkasında görmeli" (One should see the girl behind the bridesveil, the bride behind the cradle). Women are dependent upon men: "Kadının şamdanı altın olsa, mumu dikecek erkektir" (Even if woman's candle-holder is from gold, it is the man who'll stick the candle); "Ana kızına taht kurar, kız bahtı kocadan arar" (Mother sets the throne for the daughter, the daughter seeks her fortune in a husband).

In the collection of proverbs studied, with the exception of those that honor mothers who bear sons, only two proverbs among a total of seventy recognized some form of female power; one was "Kadının fendi, erkeği yendi" (Woman's wiles won over the man)—not a particularly flattering recognition of women's strength—and the other was "Erkeği vezir eden de kadındır, rezil eden de" (It is the woman who makes a man either a vizier or a disgrace). To the extend that popular sayings reflect and perpetuate the values upheld in the society, Turkish culture upholds patriarchal values that legitimize male supremacy and the functional division of labor between men and women that keeps women within the confines of their homes.

PATRIARCHAL EDUCATION

In school, women are conditioned to play "women's roles." At the primary school level, even though the Ministry of National Education recognizes the equal rights of the sexes and shuns dicrimination, teachers are required for elective studies to teach knitting, sewing and embroidery to girls and mechanical skills to boys.[122] Schools are expected to carry sewing machines, ironing boards, and knitting and embroidery equipment, specified for the use of girl students.[123] The guidelines for teachers on child development elaborate how girls develop interests in cooking, child care and homemaking while boys enjoy technical games. The teachers are alerted that the two sexes have different interests, which should be recognized and accepted.[124]

Similarly, at the high school level, girls are encouraged to take electives in home economics, sewing, and cooking and boys to concentrate on technical subjects, including wood carving and technical repair work.[125] It is assumed that regardless of the education they receive, women will play the "women's roles" and men, the "men's roles."

PATRIARCHY IN THE MEDIA

The press and the media are other means whereby patriarchal values are reflected and perpetuated. Despite gradually changing trends, literary works depict the subordinate status of women.[126] Popular magazines, and women's journals, such as *Elele* (Hand in Hand) or *Kadın* (Woman), reinforce women's place in the home. A systematic study of literature, news, films, and advertisements to discover the extent to which they still reflect and propagate women's subordinate status is not within the scope of this work; however, some examples of an earlier decade or two, which were the frames of reference of women we shall study, might illustrate the point.

Hayat (Life) magazine's interviews with the wives of prominent politicians reflects the prevailing patriarchal values in the society. Mrs. Atıfet Sunay, the wife of the former Turkish President Cevdet Sunay, sends the following message to Turkish women, at the end of an interview: "I advise them (Turkish women) to shun extremist behaviors, not to abandon humility, to be sacrificing wives closely interested in their homes and good, careful mothers who try to rear honest patriotic sons useful to their countries. I found happiness in devotion to my husband and children.[127]

There is no doubt that child rearing is a most significant task in the society. Yet Mrs. Sunay's message emphasizes more than the significance of child raising. Her message is a promotion of the traditional women's role in line with a patriarchal division of labor where women take care of the household duties and men run the public world: it is of no consequence that domestic duties close off alternative options women might want to choose to secure the public recognition. The wife of the former Republican People's Party (RPP) president, Rahşan Ecevit, conceded that although she might be an equal partner with her husband, "there is only one breadwinner who earns the family income, so of course one has to go along with him."[128] The *Hayat* interviewer concluded "that Mrs. Ecevit is an ideal Turkish woman who abides by Turkish traditions and is aware of Western traditions." The conclusion that can be drawn is that the ideal Turkish woman propagated by popular magazines such as *Hayat* is the supportive housewife who knows, and is proud of, her subordinate status in relation to her husband.

The rootedness of patriarchal values in society becomes more evident when there is the possibility of a challenge to these values. In 1981, when the Civil Code Commission, after several years, proposed conceding a woman's right to use her maiden name and the abolition of the clause, "the husband is the head of the family" from the Civil Code, the Turkish public—generally silent on political issues—was suddenly politicized, expressing its resentment in the press.[129] In an interview with the politically moderate daily *Milliyet*, ex-admiral Bülent Ulusu, the prime minister of the 1980–83 junta that prided itself on its Kemalist heritage, expressed his opposition to the proposal—which has not been accepted to this day—as follows: "The male, regardless of what the Civil Code says, is the head of the family as the tradition of the Turkish nation dictates. Nations live by their traditions and laws should be made in compliance with those traditions . . . the proposal will inevitably come before us in the Cabinet meeting. . . . My personal opinion on this subject is definite. The head of the family is clearly the man. In the Cabinet meeting, I will express my opposition to the proposal decisively."[130]

Overview

When we review the historical development of patriarchy in Turkey, we see the changing nature of male domination in society. Women formally secluded from men in the urban Ottoman society have legal access to economic and political power in the Turkish Republic. Yet beyond the issue of formal legal seclusion, at a more substantive level, lack of education coupled with economic dependence on men prevent women from challenging the strict functional division of labor between the sexes. To this day, men's power in the public realm and formal authority in the family prevails. Half of Turkey's women as opposed to a quarter of its men are illiterate. Only about a third of the primary and secondary school graduates and one fifth of the university graduates are women. Even though women make up 36 percent of the labor force, more than 90 percent of women in the labor force are in the agricultural sector working as unpaid family laborers.

Within the family, both men and women agree that the husband is the ultimate authority. The society in general upholds patriarchal values. Common sayings and maxims exalt allegedly such masculine virtues as economic independence and autonomy. Literary works reflect the predicament of the subjugated woman confined to her traditional wife/mother role. Popular magazines encourage women to accept their subjugation. Even public educational institutions assume that women play the traditional women's roles that deny them public authority.

The interesting aspect of this patriarchal scene is that men rather than women initiated the transition from the Ottoman to the Turkish patriarchy. Although the question of women's rights might have been a means rather than an end for the founders of the Turkish Republic, it was nevertheless through the efforts of these men that legal inequalities were largely abolished and women's rights to participate in public life recognized. It is within this context, where men promoted women's rights and where man-made reforms provide women opportunities as well as constraints, that we shall discuss politics and office holding by women.

3
Politics and Office Holding by Women

Political systems shape the nature of political office holding by women. Who holds what type of political office under what conditions depends on the rules of the political game as well as socio-economic variables or psychological factors. Social scientists study the relationship between different types of electoral systems and women's election to political office.[1] Party ideologies are correlated to womens' political office holding.[2] In this chapter, I shall introduce the women elected to political office in the context of the Turkish political system. My aim is to observe how social or political institutions are structured to shape women's election to office. Do they facilitate or hinder women's political aspirations? To what extent do the man-made institutions of the Republic provide women opportunities as well as constraints to success in political life.

I shall first present the development of the Turkish political system, delineating the crucial stages from its foundation in 1923 up to the 1980 military coup. In this context, I shall focus on the qualifications of women legislators to determine how typical they were. I shall then compare the women legislators with other women who hold political office at the local level in the municipality councils.

The Turkish Political System

THE ELECTED MEMBERS OF PARLIAMENT (MPS)

In 1923, the Grand National Assembly declared the Turkish state a republic. From 1923 to 1980 the republic went through two phases marked by the constitutional changes of the post-1960 military coup. Between 1923 and 1960, a unicameral assembly called the Grand National Assembly served as the national legislature; the 1961 constitution installed a bicameral system with a lower house, called the National Assembly, and an upper house, the Senate.[3]

Within this formal political structure, an authoritarian single-party system was replaced by a multiparty democracy. In the first constitutional period from 1923 to 1946, the military-bureaucratic cadre who founded the republic governed Turkey. During this so-called single-party era, under the aegis of the Republican Peoples' Party (RPP), Mustafa Kemal maintained a firm grip over the national legislature until his death in 1938. His successor, İsmet İnönü, governed the country along the lines defined by Kemal until 1946. Deputies were chosen to the Grand National Assembly in a two-level election system. The RPP appointed, rather than elected, deputies. In the absence of an opposition party, a list of the RPP candidates, each with a petition that carried 300 voter signatures nominating the candidate, would be presented to the party delegates who then made the final choice of representatives.[4] In an era when Kemal and the RPP enjoyed uncontested power in politics, deputies were their chosen men.

Between 1946 and 1960, a transition occurred to a multiparty system under the surveillance of İnönü. The Democratic Party (DP), established in 1946 to represent those dissatisfied with or ignored under the RPP rule, came to power in 1950. During the multiparty era, representatives to the National Assembly were elected on a majority system. Voters chose from the list of candidates prepared by the two parties. In each election province, the party with more votes sent its total list of candidates to the National Assembly. In each electoral district, which corresponded to each province in the country, the party leadership was still very influential in the preparation of candidacy lists.[5]

After a year of military rule following the 1960 coup, the bicameral Grand National Assembly went into effect under the 1961 constitution. The new election laws, based on the proportional representation system, encouraged the formation of new parties. Under this system, each party sent representatives to the parliament in proportion to the number of votes it received. Except for the 1965–71 period, when the Justice Party (JP), which inherited the DP electorate, had decisive power, the post-1960 period was an era of weak coalitions. Each party had its candidacy list for the elections, prepared under procedures determined by its own party statute in its primary elections.[6] The party delegates voted in the primary elections to determine the candidacy lists upon which the electorate then voted.

LOCAL LEVEL

At the local level, provincial governments and municipalities provide the platform for politics and administration. "Vilayets," provincial governments, are governed by a "vali," governor, appointed by the national government. The vali presides over the provincial council, which is elected by general vote in each province. Hence the provincial government is directly responsible both to the national government and to the local electorate.

The municipality, although still under the control of the Ministry of the Interior, is more accountable to the local electorate than is the provincial government. Unlike the vali, the major (belediye başkanı) as well as the municipality council, are elected by popular vote. The special status of the vali of Istanbul, which enabled him to serve as the head of both the provincial and the municipal governments, was abolished after 1960. At the local level, municipality elections are a microcosm of the political competition for parliamentary seats at the national level.

PARTY STRUCTURE AND WOMEN

Political parties are the backbone of the Turkish political system. Before the 1980 military intervention, the General Congress, the Central Executive Committee, disciplinary bodies, parliamentary groups, and youth and women's organizations, listed in terms of their statutory powers, constituted the central organs of Turkish parties.[8] This formal organization, which describes post-1960, pre-1980 political parties, has developed since the beginning of the multiparty period.

Our concern being women in Turkish politics, it is necessary to draw attention to the Woman's Branches (WB) of the main parties. From the mid-1950s until 1980, after which the WB were banned, the two major parties had separate organizational units subsidiary to their main cadres through which they expected women to participate in politics.[9] The WB were subject to the arbitration of the main branches and financially dependent on them. As subsidiary branches, they aimed to spread the party ideology defined by the main cadres. Their programs reveal their subsidiary status.

In the WB program of the JP, the responsibilities of the subsidiary branches appeared in the following order:

1. To recruit JP partisans
2. To try to develop and strengthen a Western style democratic order
3. To work for the realization of the welfare state
4. To work for the protection of the family that is the pillar of the society

5. To try to encourage Turkish women to participate in social and political life
6. To enable the Turkish women to assume responsibility in the progress and development of social and political life[10]

The fact that the many goals of the WB might be contradictory never seems to come up as an issue: the WB is expected first to mobilize JP support among women, then to encourage women to perpetuate their traditional roles within the family, and finally to encourage women to partake in political and social life. Yet clearly, protection for the family in its traditional form where women do the homemaking may prevent women from actively participating in political life.

The program of the RPP's WB was similar. Even though the RPP WB program does express commitment to women's rights and Kemalist reforms, promotion of political women is not an explicit priority. In order of appearance, the WB of the RPP claims as its responsibilities:

1. To organize meetings and talks
2. To publish brochures and magazines
3. To make visits to villages to enlighten women citizens
4. To spread the party program and increase membership, especially of women
5. As a subsidiary branch, to help the main party organization[11]

In neither of the WB programs was the promotion of women's rights seriously endorsed. The issue of women's effective office holding was not even raised.

Political Representatives

THE ELECTED MEMBERS OF PARLIAMENT

Within the Turkish political system as sketched above, politicians with certain credentials were elected to represent the people. Like many other political elites, they have a high educational and occupational status.[12] Frey, in *The Turkish Political Elite*, delineates three characteristics of the parliamentary representatives. The typical representative to the National Assembly is an adult Turk who has some claim to intellectual status, an official occupational status, and a fairly powerful local community position.[13] The educational levels of the representatives have been consistently high over the different stages of the republic.[14] About 70 to 80 percent of the Parliament since the foundation of the Republic had a university education. The representatives, as a highly educated group, also had claims to official occupational status.

However, the nature of the occupational status changed over the years. During the single-party era, military men, bureaucrats and teachers—all representatives of the state in some way—made up the majority in the Parliament. During the multiparty era, professionals—doctors, engineers and especially lawyers—outnumbered the officials and other occupational groups. That trend continued into the 1980s. Members from business, trade, commerce and agriculture increased during the multiparty era, their total number becoming more than that of the officials, yet less than that of the professionals. As the power of the military bureaucratic cadre eroded, the officials vacated their seats to the professionals, especially lawyers.[15]

Frey refers to the third typical characteristic of Turkish MPs, that is, their role as representatives of the province in which they were born, as "localism." The localist trend fluctuated in strength over the years. In the 1920s, about 62 percent of the deputies were born in the province they represented. As the military bureaucratic cadre established its power in Parliament, however, localism diminished to the point where about 30 to 40 percent of the deputies were representatives of their own province. When the multiparty era began, the number of deputies who represented the province in which they were born increased again, rising to 70 percent in the 1960s and continuing to increase in the 1970s.[16]

In summary, during the single-party era when the military bureaucratic cadres were in power and the party leadership had firm control over the party, to be elected to the Parliament one had either to be part of the party leadership, or at least be approved by it. The political elite was a closed group. Access to it through other channels was difficult. During the RPP-DP era before the 1960 coup, the two parties increasingly recruited candidates from educated professionals who had provincial roots rather than from the official representatives of the state, such as the bureaucracy or the military. After 1960, the rules of the game changed again. The elected candidates were not only educated professionals but also party workers who were vote-getters among the delegates. In the metropolitan areas, prospective candidates worked in the party ranks; in the rural regions, they established patron-client relations under the protection of their respective political parties.[17] However,

Table 7
Women in the Parliament, 1935–1980
NATIONAL ASSEMBLY

	Term	Number of Women in the Parliament	Women as % of total
1935–39	V	18	4.5
1939–43	VI	15	3.7
1943–46	VII	16	3.7
1946–50	VIII	9	1.9
1950–54	IX	3	0.6
1954–57	X	4	0.7
1957–60	XI	8	1.3
1961–65	1	3	0.7
1965–69	2	8	1.7
1969–73	3	5	1.1
1973–77	4	6	1.3
1977–80	5	4	0.9
TOTAL		99	

SENATE

	Term	Number of Women in the Parliament	Women as % of total
1961–65	1	2	1.3
1965–69	2	3	2
1969–73	3	3	2
1973–77	4	3	2
1977–81	5	3	2
TOTAL		14	

CONSTITUTIVE ASSEMBLY

1960–61		4	1.4

despite the challenge of the 1960 coup to the DP, a tradition of a two-party political system with two different political constituencies was established.

THE ELECTED WOMEN POLITICIANS: NATIONAL LEGISLATURES

Since 1934 when women's suffrage was granted, the women elected to Parliament never constituted more than 4.5 percent of its membership. The percentage of elected women steadily declined from the figure of 4.5 percent in the 1935–39 Parliament to levels of less than 1 percent. The ruling elite of the single party era that initiated suffrage was responsible for the relatively high percentage of female representatives in earlier times because they consciously appointed women to Parliament. Table 7 shows the percentage of women elected to the Parliament in each election period between 1935 and 1980.[18] Sixty-four women occupied a total of ninety-nine seats in the National Assembly while eight women occupied a total of fourteen seats in the Senate. Changes in the electoral system in 1960 from a majority to a proportional representation system did not radically alter patterns of women's representation in the multiparty period.

In a society where higher education and official occupational status are necessary credentials for election to Parliament but where only about a fifth or a sixth of the university graduates, about a fifth of the lawyers, and a third of the teachers are women, other things being equal, we can expect fewer women to be elected to office than men. Compared to such other Middle Eastern countries as Jordan, Kuwait, Saudi Arabia, and Yemen, in which women have neither the right to vote nor to run for office, Turkey, which recognized both these rights for women in 1935, had at least some women elected to the Parliament.[19] Yet, the dictates of high level office holding worked against women in Turkey.

THE LOCAL LEVEL: MUNICIPALITY COUNCILS

The Istanbul and Ankara municipality council records to which I had access show that the proportion of female representatives in these councils was higher than that for the National Assembly. Table 8 presents the number of women members in the Istanbul and Ankara municipality councils.[20]

Table 8
Women in the Metropolitan Municipality Councils

	Istanbul		Ankara	
	Number of women/ Total membership	% of women	Number of women/ Total membership	% of women
1963	6/93	6.4	5/57	8.7
1968	10/102	9.8	9/72	12.5
1973	9/117	7.7	9/81	11.0
1977	7/133	5.2	10/103	9.7

In the Istanbul Municipality Council (MC), 24 women occupied a total of 32 seats, while in Ankara 27 women held a total of 33 seats. Even though the percentages of women in these municipalities were higher than in the National Assembly, these figures do not indicate a rising trend.

THE WOMEN MPS

The 64 female MPs elected since 1935 have background characteristics similar to the male MPs. Both groups are highly educated professionals. The specific nature of the professionalism among female MPs changes depending on the era in which they were elected to Parliament, an observation which holds equally for male MPs. Tables 9 and 10 show the educational and occupational backgrounds of women who have been elected to the Parliament in different political eras.[21]

Table 9
Educational Backgrounds of Women MPs

	Single party 1935–46		Multiparty 1946–60		Multiparty 1960–80		Total		Senate (1960–1980)
	*	%	*	%	*	%	*	%	
University	29	59	14	58	17	65	60	60	14
Senior high	14	28.5	10	42	9	34	33	33	
Junior high	5	10					5	5	
Elementary									
None	1	2					1	1	
TOTAL	49		24		26		99		14

* number of women
% percent of total woman

Table 10
Occupational Backgrounds of Women MPs

	Single party 1935–46		Multiparty 1946–60		Multiparty 1960–80		Total		Senate (1960–1980)
	*	%	*	%	*	%	*	%	*
Law			3	12.5	9	34.6	12	12	3
Medicine	5	10	1	4			6	6	
Teaching	32	65	13	54	9	34.6	54	54	2
Housewife					3	11.5	3	3	
Other	12	24	7	29	5	19	24	24	9
TOTAL	49		24		26		99		14

As these tables show, roughly 60 percent of all women elected to the National Assembly (22) had a university education. Recalling that about 70 and 80 percent of the elected MPs had university degrees, the educational qualifications of the female MPs almost equal those of the male MPs. Contrary to what has been claimed elsewhere, women parliamentarians are not better educated than the male MPs;[23] however, in a country where the illiteracy rate runs at 50 percent of the female population, and where as late as 1975 only 16 percent of university graduates were women, female politicians, 60 percent of whom have higher education, are clearly from an educational elite.

In terms of occupational status, again the female MPs are much like the male MPs, although very different from typical Turkish women. As the table on occupational status indicates, in the single party era when the officials—namely the military officers, bureaucrats and teachers, and state employees propagating Kemalist ideology—made up about 35 to 55 percent of the MPs, roughly 60 percent of the female MPs were teachers. In the multiparty era, the professionals held about 40 to 45 percent of the seats. Fifteen to 20 percent of the female parliamentarians were professionals, especially lawyers. In later years this figure rose to 35 percent. In a society where 90 percent of women in the labor force are employed in agriculture, the professionals among the female politicians (15 to 35 percent) are not representative of Turkish women with regard to occupational status. However, the female MPs are quite representative of elected parliamentarians. The majority of those recruited are male; male credentials set the criteria for recruitment. Hence, only those women who have the same credentials as men survive the competition for political office. Women are at a clear disadvantage in assuming political office, because only a minority have the credentials that men do.

The female MPs who were similar in education and professional status to the male MPs were generally not representatives for the provinces in which they were born, unlike the increasing number of male MPs. Between 1930 and 1970, about 50 percent of the male MPs represented the provinces in which they were born. For the same period, only 24 of a total number of 99 seats occupied by women were held by women for the provinces in which they were born. This low incidence of localism among the female politicians is understandable in light of the higher levels of female education and professionalism in metropolitan areas from which the female politicians are generally elected, regardless of their place of birth.

THE WOMEN MUNICIPALITY COUNCIL MEMBERS

Data on women elected to municipality councils is limited. A comprehensive listing of the MC memberships in Turkey could not be.

found, and access to the MC records that document the proceedings of the sessions was denied. On the basis of the post-1960 Istanbul Municipality Council records that were available, it appears that women elected to municipality councils are different from those elected to the national legislatures both in terms of their educational and occupational status and also in their political interest—but that cannot decisively be judged without access to records of the MC proceedings. The women on the municipality councils were both less educated and less professional than those in the National Legislature. Tables 11 and 12 show the educational and occupational status of the female municipality council members in the post-1960 Istanbul MCs.[24]

Table 11
Educational Background of Women MC Members in Istanbul

	1963		1968		1973		1977		Total	
	*	%	*	%	*	%	*	%	*	%
University	3	50	3	30	2	22	2	29	10	31
Senior high	1	16	3	30	1	11	1	14	6	19
Junior high	2	33	3	30	6	66	4	57	15	47
Elementary			1	10					1	3
TOTAL	6	99	10	100	9	99	7	100	32	100

* number of women
% percent of total women

Table 12
Occupational Background of Women MC Members in Istanbul

	1963		1968		1973		1977		Total	
	*	%	*	%	*	%	*	%	*	%
Lawyer			2	20	1	11	1	14	4	12
Medical dr.	1	16							1	3
Teacher	2	33	1	10	1	11			4	12
Housewife	3	50	7	70	7	77	5	71	22	70
Other							1	14	1	3
TOTAL	6	99	10	100	9	99	7	99	32	100

* number of women
% percent of total women

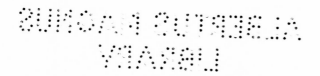

As these tables indicate, about one-third of female MC members, in contrast to two-thirds of female MPs, are university educated. Fifty percent of MC members terminated their education at junior and senior high school. This was true for only 5 percent of women MPs.

The lower educational status of the female MC members is clearly reflected in their occupations. Seventy percent of female MC members are housewives; the majority of female MPs are professionals. The total percentage of lawyers, doctors and teachers among the female MC members studied is 27 percent, as opposed to 72 percent among the MPs. The women MC members thus are more representative of Turkish women in terms of educational and occupational status than are the highly educated and professional female MPs. Insofar as fewer educated and professional women have been elected to the MCs, women appear less disadvantaged in competing at this level than at the parliamentary level.

MARITAL STATUS: MPS AND MC MEMBERS

Most of the female politicians, although not a clear majority, are married women, and they usually have children. During the single-party era, 57 percent of the female MPs were married at the time they assumed office; the proportion increased to 62 percent during the multi-party era prior to 1960, and to 80 percent after 1960. Table 13 shows the figures on marital status in more detail.[25]

Table 13
Marital Status of Female MPs

	Married		Widowed		Single		With children/ married	
	*	%	*	%	*	%	*	%
Single party	28/49	57	9/49	18	12/49	25	22/37	60
1946–60	15/24	62	3/24	13	6/24	25	13/18	72
1960–80	21/26	80	3/26	12	2/26	8	24/24	100
TOTAL	64/99	64	15/99	15	20/99	20		

* number of women/total women
% percent of total women

Among those women elected to the Istanbul Municipality Council since 1960, only 50 percent were married at the time they were elected to office. The figures changed as follows.[26]

Table 14
Marital Status of Female MC Members in Istanbul

	Married		Single		Widow	
	*	%	*	%	*	%
1963	2/6	33	2/6	33	2/6	33
1968	4/10	40	3/10	30	3/10	30
1973	4/9	44	2/9	22	3/9	33
1977	6/7	85	1/7	15	0/7	0
TOTAL	16/32	50	8/32	25	8/32	25

* number of women/total women
% percent of total women

Although most female politicians are married, if we exclude widows from their number their majority is not a large one. In total, 64 percent of the MPs and 50 percent of the Istanbul MC members were married when they assumed office. In 1963, only 33 percent of the MC members, and in 1968, 40 percent of the MC members were married women. Even though we are talking about just a few women, it is quite significant that among these few, only a small proportion were married.

PARTY AFFILIATION: MPS AND MC MEMBERS

Both the educated, professional, mostly married female MPs elected since the beginning of the multiparty era in 1946, as well as the less educated, less professional, but still mostly married female MC members from Istanbul have mainly represented the RPP. Prior to 1946, elected women were all representatives of the RPP, the single ruling party that promoted suffrage. From 1946 to 1960, there were 11 female representatives from the RPP as opposed to 12 from the DP. The large number of female representatives (18, 15 and 16 in the 5th, 6th and 7th terms respectively) the RPP could promote during its single-party rule sharply decreased once there was political competition. Between 1960 and 1980, the RPP had 10, while the JP which replaced the DP had 11 representatives. After 1946, the RPP had a total of 21 female MPs. The DP and JP together had a total of 23 female MPs. Table 15 shows the party affiliations of the female representatives in each election term.[27]

If we disregard the single-party rule of the RPP, parties of the center right, that is, the DP together with the JP and the party of the center left, RPP seem to have promoted about the same number of women parliamentarians (twenty-three, as opposed to twenty-one, respectively), during the same time period. In other words, there does not seem to be a strong correlation between party ideologies and political representation of women.

Table 15
Party Affiliation of the Female MPs

Terms	8 1946–50	9 50–54	10 54–57	11 57–60	1 61–65	2 65–69	3 69–73	4 73–77	5 77–80	Total
RPP (CHP)*	9	1		1		3	2	3	2	21
DP (DP)		1	4	7						12
JP (AP)					2	3	2	2	2	11
RPNP (CKMP)					1					1
NTP (YTP)						1				1
TLP (TIP)						1				1
NP (MP)							1			1
DP (DP 2)								1		1
Independent		1								1

* See Appendix for key to party names

At the local level, since 1960, the Istanbul MC women representatives were predominantly members of the RPP. Out of a total of thirty-two female representatives elected to the MC in 1963, 1968, 1973 and 1977, twenty-six were from the RPP, while only four were from the JP and two from the TLP. The figures for each election period are shown in Table 16.

Table 16
Party Affiliations of Female MC Members in Istanbul

	1963	1968	1973	1977	Total
RPP (CHP)	3	8	8	7	26
JP (AP)	3		1		4
TLP (TIP)		2			2
TOTAL	6	10	9	7	32

In 1968, the JP was disqualified from participation in the Istanbul MC elections for infraction of the rules; the RPP representatives might not have been as numerous had the JP taken part in those elections. But even when we discount the 1968 elections, female representatives from the RPP outnumber those from other parties.

Overview

Unlike many Western countries, in which proportional representation tends to facilitate women's move into parliaments,[28] a correlation between the electoral system of proportional representation and women's election to political office is not seen in Turkey. For reasons discussed before, the highest percentage of women in the Turkish Parliament is during the autocratic single-party era when women were practically appointed to their seats. The percentages continued to remain low as the electoral system changed from one based on majority system to proportional representation during the multiparty era.

When we turn our attention to other contextual factors that might be critical in shaping women's access to political power, we see that electoral chances of women are highly dependent on their status in their respective parties. In a system with list vote, as is the case in Turkey, parties decide which candidates are to be elected when they prepare the candidacy lists. In a system of proportional representation, the ranking of candidates on the list is critical for ensuring election. While the number of votes the party gets determines how many candidates will be selected, the higher up one is on the list the better the candidate's chances of election. The question that needs to be pursued is why women do not or can not become strong candidates nominated by their parties.

A major obstacle for success is women's lack of qualifications. In a society where the typical MP is a highly educated professional, women are clearly disadvantaged as potential candidates because they are, in general, neither as educated nor as professionally qualified as men. In other words, rules of the game work against women. Nevertheless, women elected to Parliament are very similar to their male colleagues in terms of educational and professional qualifications. Only at the local level, in municipality councils, do the less educated housewives get elected to political office.

Turkish data present no strong support for the connection between marital status and electoral success, either. Although a majority of the women politicians, MPs as well as MC members, were married, those who were single (including widows) were nonetheless a large minority. In regards to party affiliation, slightly more women represented the social democratic RPP than the more conservative DP and its post-1960 outgrowth, JP, in the Parliament as well as in the municipality councils studied. However, at the parliamentary level, discounting women elected to Parliament during the single-party era of the RPP, the discrepancy in party affiliation was not significant. It would be difficult to generalize that the center left parties had a propensity to have more women representatives in politics. Other factors seem to be relevant in explaining how and why some women do enter politics and succeed and others do not.

4
Who Are the Women Politicians?

As Gaetano Mosca perceptively put it,

> Ruling minorities are usually so constituted that the individuals who make them up are distinguished from the mass of the governed by qualities that give them a certain material, intellectual or even moral superiority.[1]

To the extent that the women politicians studied belong to a "ruling minority," they are distinguished from the mass of the governed, not merely by their high educational and professional standing, but by other qualities as well. In fact, those elected to the municipality councils are not necessarily professional or highly educated people. Beyond the educational qualifications, ideological orientations or marital status of the women politicians elected to political office, what are the qualities that distinguish them from the mass of the governed? What are their family background, economic standings or the authority structures in their families? To pursue these questions beyond published material, I shall draw on my interviews with a group of male and female politicians. More specifically, I shall move beyond the macro level institutional factors to consider variables at the micro level that might be crucial in shaping women's election to political office. My focus is on the patriarchal organization of their personal lives that could support as well as obstruct access to the public realm.

The Interviews and Sample

SELECTION OF SAMPLE

The main focus of this study is on women parliamentarians. Forty women were elected to the Turkish Parliament during the multi-party era (1950–80).[2] I compiled a list of the female deputies (MPs) from the parliamentary albums and reached as many of them as was possible through personal contacts or publicly available records such as telephone directories. Some were not available, others declined to be interviewed. Of the forty, I was able to interview eighteen.[3] The first two interviews were used in order to develop the interview schedule and, consequently, excluded from the sample.

I also interviewed a sample of ten male members of the National Assembly. The purpose of these interviews was to provide a perspective on the responses of the female representatives. Unlike the female representatives, there were many male parliamentarians from which to choose. Since the sixteen female MPs interviewed were from metropolitan centers, to facilitate a comparison of career patterns, I restricted the male sample to those elected from Istanbul after 1960. The sample was further restricted by the choice of election years in which both men and women were elected to office. This particular selection meant that the male representatives interviewed, unlike many others, competed against female candidates. Hence, these men were rivals and colleagues who presumably could form their attitudes toward women in politics from personal experience. Between 1960 and 1980 seventy-two men held ninety-five parliamentary seats from Istanbul.[4] As with the women, I tried to contact and interview as many men as I could.

For the municipality council sample, I used the lists of the Istanbul and Ankara MC members elected after 1960. Of the fifty-one women elected, I was able to interview twelve.

In the three samples, random selection was not possible because of the limitation in the numbers of those that were available or prepared to be interviewed. However, since the universes were quite homogeneous, those interviewed were representative of their respective universes in terms of educational and occupational background. The issue is further discussed in Appendix C.

The Interviews

The interviews consisted mostly of taped discussions.[5] The tape recorder was used at the discretion of the respondents, which meant that I turned it off when they asked me not to record some of their responses and, on some occasions, not use the tape at all.

Unlike many of the men who asked to be interviewed in their offices, most of the women invited me to their homes. Due to the military government's ban on political activity, none of those interviewed were politically active at the time of the interviews. Unlike the men who had to continue to earn their living, most of the women were "at home." Usually, I had longer interviews with the women than with the men, most probably because I did not feel comfortable interviewing in offices when I was constantly aware that these men had engagements to meet and calls to respond to. However, once I was able to obtain an interview appointment, all the politicians whom I interviewed, male as well as female, were very responsive to my questions and seemed to enjoy talking about themselves and their experiences. I was a sympathetic listener, nodding and expressing interest and assuring the respondents of their anonymity rather than maintaining a noncommital, objective stance.

Economic Status

The significance of personal economic means is undeniable for an aspiring politician; money helps in getting oneself recognized, whether in responding to voters or contributing to party funds. In a society where one has to be an educated professional to be an MP— as the increasing numbers of educated professional representatives indicate—one also needs money to acquire the right education. As could be expected, perhaps in the light of their high educational and occupational status, MPs whom I interviewed all considered themselves to come from economically secure, middle class families. Female MPs seemed to come from relatively more affluent families than the men.

Economic resources are less significant for holding political office at the local level. The aspiring political candidate needs to spend less time and money to gain acceptance in her own district (ilçe); there are fewer delegates to influence, fewer needs to which to respond, and hence a smaller financial burden. On the other hand, once elected, the MC members (MCMs), unlike the MPs, receive only token salaries. Therefore, to be a MC member one needs less money to be elected, yet one must have sufficient independent means to maintain oneself in office. Compared with the woman MPs, the women elected to the MC come from economically less affluent families. Table 17 summarizes the politicians' answers concerning the economic status of their parents' families.

Table 17
Parental Economic Status

	Female MPs	Male MPs	Female MCMs
Upper Middle Class	7	1	
Middle Class	9	4	6
Lower Middle Class		5	4
Lower Class			2
TOTAL	16	10	12

As in the traditional patriarchal family, with the exception of two women MPs whose mothers worked as well, the fathers of these politicians earned the family income. Regardless of any other means of income, the high occupational status of the female MPs' fathers ensured that the families would be at least middle class. There were professionals, high level bureaucrats, high ranking military officers and a businessman among the fathers of the female MPs. In contrast, the fathers of the male MPs were lower-level bureaucrats, artisans, elementary school teachers, and a businessman. There were many (5 of the 12) lower-level military officers among the fathers of the women MC members. A few of them were small businessmen (2 of the 12), and teachers (2 of the 12). There was one bureaucrat and one worker.

All those interviewed saw themselves as financially better off than their parents. More women MPs considered themselves to be upper middle class compared to their parents. Similarly, more male MPs and female MC members considered themselves middle class rather than lower middle class. Table 18 shows their responses.

Table 18
Economic Status of Politicians

	Female MPs	Male MPS	Female MCMs
Upper Middle Class	9	3	2
Middle Class	7	7	7
Lower Middle Class			3
TOTAL	16	10	12

Among the women MPs, six were married to professionals (such as doctors and lawyers), two to top-level bureaucrats, one to a former head of the armed forces, and two to eminent MPs. As discussed earlier, the female MPs themselves were a group of highly professional women; they all lived in the best parts of Istanbul and Ankara and, with one exception, owned at least the apartment in which they lived. It is no surprise that these women considered themselves economically well off.

Most of the male MPs were the sole breadwinners in their families. There were two exceptions, one wife of an MP worked as a bank clerk and another wife taught at a girls' vocational school; however, both wives assumed lower status jobs than their husbands. Thus, since the male MPs, unlike the women, in most cases are the sole wage earners in their families, their slightly less affluent economic status is understandable. Nevertheless, we are talking about only slight differences in economic status. With one exception, all the male MPs, like the women MPs owned, at least one apartment floor in the best part of town. Most of them had their own business offices, rented though not necessarily owned, in the busiest commercial districts.

The married female MC members, most of whom were housewives, had husbands with occupations that would carry modest incomes. Among the ten MC members who were married, two were divorced and two were widows. Two had husbands with high-status occupations (a doctor and a governor), the other husbands were small businessmen. While the MC members with whom I talked in Ankara lived in the popular, expensive parts of the city, the Istanbul MC members often lived in more modest homes.

ECONOMIC PROBLEMS IN POLITICS

The Turkish government closely regulated campaign propaganda. The party rather than the individual candidate was allotted a fixed time on the state-controlled Turkish Radio Television (TRT). The places and the types of posters that political parties could display and the public speeches they could make were supervised by law. The state regulation of election campaigns curbed the tendency to spend excessive amounts of money in elections.

However, funding was needed in order to reach the electorate and to pay party dues. Most of the women MPs interviewed said that they did not have economic problems. They had cash reserves and surplus income to spend on campaign expenses. One woman did say that she had to borrow money and another said that she had to sell property in order to acquire the requisite funds. Most of the women used their own cars rather than sharing or renting them in the campaign. More male MPs (4 of 10), as opposed to women (1 of 16) said that they had economic problems while campaigning. Other male MPs (3 of 10) responded to the same question saying "not really". Among those who said that they did not have economic problems, two explained that their economic problems were relieved by the support they had from associations, such as the labor unions or the Cab Drivers/Cab Owners Association that they represented, and without whose support they would have had significant problems.

Although the female MC members were slightly less affluent then the MPs, in the context of their local political involvement, they did not have significant economic problems while campaigning. A few (2 of 12) said they did have economic problems and others (2 of 12) responded with "not really." Most of them (8 of 12) said they did not have any economic problems. In fact, most (9 of 12), unlike most female MPs (13 of 16) and a number of male MPs (4 of 10), did not own cars to use in the electoral campaign.

We can say that only those women who would not incur economic difficulties held office, while many men who would have economic problems still ran for office and successfully overcame them. It seems that most women were either unable to overcome economic problems or did not even volunteer for candidacy when they did not have the funds.

For an idea of the economic expenses of an aspiring political candidate, we may quote Handan Yavaş, a lower middle class MC member, who indicated that she clearly had economic problems in her political career as well as in the campaigns.[6] Handan Yavaş explained as follows,

> Our financial troubles were many, many. We did not have our own means of transportation. A few friends had their own cars, but we had problems of transportation. You need cars to reach the people. We organized special nights, circumcision ceremonies, dinners (for the RPP); but the income from these was not enough (for the party to subsidize the candidates); you badly needed money especially in the election times if you meant to be elected. We sacrificed a lot. I know many times when we had to curb our private concerns, pool our money, cooperate and act together. And also, more importantly, you organize dinners and things for the party but you need clothes to wear and tickets to buy for these occasions. I was never one who cared for clothes and things, but you still need a lot of money to get yourself accepted.

As Handan Yavaş suggests, the candidate not only needs to reach the electorate or raise party funds, but also to attend dinners, buy tickets, and wear the right clothes. Raising party funds or campaigning for the party does not even necessarily mean promoting one's personal ambitions for office. A person like Yavaş who does not have the means is acutely conscious of the expenses. Her experience tells us that those female politicians, most of whom do not complain of economic problems, have the means.

In contrast to Yavaş, the answers given by most of the upper middle class or middle class female MPs and the middle class or even lower middle class MC members were as follows: the RPP MP Tülin Sağlam, like many other respondents, curtly stated that she is from the middle class. When asked if she had any economic problems, she responded, "No, not at all; for I came to political office using very little money." At the local level, the RPP MC member Belkıs

Nil contended that political involvement is not that costly. She answered,

> No, I spent no money from my pocket to make myself known. This is a small place anyway. You cannot have money games here. When we had to give speeches etc., my friends from the party, some had cars, we used them.

Olcay Fen, a JP MC member who served in the Ankara MC for several terms, emphasized that not only were the expenses necessary for political involvement small, but that she had the money. She noted,

> I didn't have any economic problems. Of course the membership dues, party fees, transportation costs all went out of our pocket at the time; but I had the means. They weren't a burden to me.

The male MPs, unlike the female politicians, emphasized the financial problems they had in getting elected. The male MPs needed financial support and they successfully got it. For example, the RPP MP Osman Dur had to borrow money:

> There were many financial problems. I became indebted about 30,000 T.L.[7] Perhaps it is not too much, but it was too much for me. I did not have the ready money to use. And I had to have this money for the bare minimum to make my trips. I did not go to the parliament taking bribes and bribing others.

Osman Dur was an aspiring young lawyer who did not have the money but was keen on becoming an MP.[8] If becoming elected meant finding the money, he would get it. Whereas Osman Dur used his personal connections to acquire the money he needed, however, the RPP MP Uğur Er had trade union support. Uğur Er was an articulate advocate of the center-left labor unions, and they provided the financial support he needed. Uğur Er explained this way,

> Financial problems, of course. In Turkey politics means money: you need men, you need money, you need a car and I had none. I was a young lawyer working for a trade union. The workers inspired me and the workers supported me; they did it all with their own initiative, not my own money. And the youth organizations supported me. They had faith in me and said, "We need him as our representative so we shall support him."

A final example is that of Osman Nuri, a RPP MP who said that his family subsidized his financial needs. He explained as follows,

Of course, there were always financial problems. I had no car. You had to hire minibuses, travel around, eat, sleep. It meant sacrifices on the part of my family. They paid for it; spent less, economized . . .

The financial problems of the male MPs were many, but they were able to make their sources of support match their needs.

To conclude, neither the female MPs nor the economically less powerful female MC members had forbidding financial problems in getting elected. What this suggests is that those women who entertained political ambitions but anticipated financial problems were either intimidated by these problems and did not even try to contest the election or were unsuccessful in raising the requisite funds and, hence, lost. Men were both less intimidated by financial constraints and were also more successful in securing funds. Only those women who started with secure finances appear to be successful in winning political office.

Authority Structure

Social scientists agree that authority structures in families affects political orientation.[9] Yet as discussed earlier they disagree on how to define or operationalize the concept.[10] Furthermore, there is disagreement on how it affects men and women differently. An attemp is made here to study the authority patterns in the politicians' families to see if they could shed light on women politicians' access to politics. The assumption is made that the question of who decides on what issues can throw light on the nature of the authority network within the family. With the focus on economic and disciplinary issues, the following questions were posed:

1. Who decides on economic questions, especially those that involve a lot of money?
2. Who is the ultimate authority concerning family discipline?

ECONOMIC DECISION MAKING IN THE PARENTS' FAMILIES

In response to the question on economic decision making, the male MPs (7 of 10) said that their fathers had the last word on economic issues. Only a fifth of the female MPs and a quarter of the MC members gave the same answer. Half the female MPs and a MC member (1 of 12) said that although ultimately it was the father who decided on economic issues, he consulted the mother before he made his decision. In contrast to none of the male MPs, four of the female MPs (4 of 16) and two (2 of 12) of the MC members said that

their parents decided together. In the families of a third of the
female MC members, mothers controlled the family budget.[11] The
female MC members' mothers had "the most say" in economic decisions compared to other mothers. Even though fathers were the sole
bread winners in the families of most politicians, the mothers of the
female politicians helped decide how to spend the family income; in
contrast, most of the male politicians' mothers let the fathers decide, or so it was claimed. Table 19 enumerates the results of this
question.

Table 19
Who Decides on Economic Issues in the Family of the Parents

	Female MPs	Male MPS	Female MC Members
Father decides	3	7	3
Father decides, but consults mother	8	2	1
Father & mother decide auton-omously on different things	1		2
Father & mother decide together	4		2
Mother decides		1	4
TOTAL	16	10	12

DISCIPLINARY DECISION MAKING IN THE PARENTS' FAMILIES

Responses to the question of "who had the final word on disciplinary issues in the family you were raised in" were similar to those on
economic decision making: the mothers of the female politicians
had more say than those of the male MPs. The male MPs without
exception considered their fathers to have been the ultimate authorities on disciplinary matters. Of the female politicians, most (12 of
16 of the MPs, 2 of 12 of the MCs) recognized their fathers as the
ultimate authoritative figures in the families, but unlike the male
MPs, qualified their answers. The typical qualifications would be:
"My father had much respect for me," "He never put his authority
to test," "He never imposed rules on us." The RPP representative
Beyhan Sunar explained:

There were set rules in the house. We were particularly respectful of our
father. We addressed him as "siz" (the polite form for "you"), always
sat down to the dinner table together with him. If one of us was late, my

father would give a stern look. We'd understand we had behaved wrong-
ly. We couldn't stay out after a certain hour at night but there was no
punishment. It just would not be approved. We could do what we
wanted within these set rules. Our father was our mentor, he was concerned with everything we did and very responsive to us.

From Sunar's response it seems clear that the family deferred to
the father's authority. His "stern look" was enough to reprimand
the children. The discipline he silently enforced was internalized
without dissent, and Beyhan Sunar was eager to convince me that
his authority was welcome. The father had the authority of a patriarch, but it was benign and protective rather than forbidding or
intimidating.

The RPP MC member Taylan Mor, on the other hand, did not
notice her father's disciplinary authority while growing up even
though she would concede he was the authoritative figure in her
family. Her response was,

I don't know. I guess father had the authority if anyone. But I grew up
in Anatolia. My father was a military officer but he did not discipline
us. I was left to do what I wanted—I was very independent, I roamed
around the hills with boys and girls. There was no one to mind our
business; we did what we wanted.

When she has to choose, Mor recognizes her father to be the
authoritative figure in the family, yet she explains she did not notice
his authority. The women politicians, unlike the male MPs, tended
to feel more comfortable with the authority of their fathers.
Whether or not it was because they internalized the patriarchal discipline at home better, they were keen to convey that it was not
intrusive. The responses to the question are in table 20.[12]

Table 20
Authority on Disciplinary Issues in the Family of the Parents

	Female MPs	Male MPS	Female MC Members
Father	4	10	2
Father, but much respect for child	9		2
Mother			2
Shared with mother	3		6
TOTAL	16	10	12

An other factor that shapes the family background of the politicians studied is religion. Islam has assumed different functions for different classes in the history of Turkish society.[13] Yet, it is generally agreed that after 1923, "the disassociation of Islam from the centers of power was complete and thorough."[14] The emerging generation of the republican elite was, accordingly, secular in its outlook. The educated, westernizing, middle and upper middle classes widely practiced Atatürk's laic principles.

All the politicians I interviewed were secular metropolitans educated to uphold Kemal's secularist and modernist reforms. They were raised in families that witnessed the War of Independence and respected Kemal. All the politicians, men and women, considered their families to be liberal on religious issues. The families made no attempt to indoctrinate the children with a religious education that could undermine the children's career aspirations.

At home, most of the parents did not perform the five daily prayers that are an obligatory rite for a practicing Muslim. Only a few fathers (three female MPs, one male MP, three female MCMs) prayed quite regularly. On the other hand, there were some women (6 of 16 MPs) whose mothers, though not fathers, performed the five daily prayers regularly. One of these mothers had made her hadj to Mecca. However, even these more pious mothers were reticent about their religious beliefs. Their daughters perceived their mothers' religious inclinations as private affairs that did not affect the daughters' career patterns.

Huriye Maslak who, unlike most politicians, did come from a family in which the father performed his five daily prayers, had this to say,

> When I was going to college, I had a talk with my father, I was curious. I asked him if our wearing bathing suits, going to the sea with our boyfriends, not praying at all, did not disturb him when he was a practicing Muslim himself. He said, "Look my child, one has to keep up with the times. . . . In my generation I was taught to express my faith this way; yours is a different generation, you follow the dictates of your time."

Maslak's father was typical, practicing his religious belief in the way he was accustomed, while conveying the message that he did not expect his daughter to imitate him. Not all the parents expressed this message orally; yet there was no misunderstanding concerning the parents' expectations of their daughters' secular inclinations.

AUTHORITY STRUCTURE WITHIN THE POLITICANS' FAMILIES

Before we discuss the authority patterns in politicians' families, the impact of marriage on their lives should be explored. Early in their marriages women politicians acquiesced to the authority of their husbands. The women rather than the men had to adapt to the demands of their married life. The male MPs unanimously said that marriage did not change their life plans; only a quarter of the female MPs and a third of the MC members thought likewise. For a majority of women, marriage meant giving up school or jobs, or being tied down with children. In short, they acquiesced to the fact that they had to steer their lives as their marriages dictated. There were none who complained. When asked if marriage altered her life plans, the RPP MP Nergis Ney responded:

> No, not really . . . Well, I guess in one sense it did. I had to quit work for a while, my kids were born and I had to look after them . . . but I resumed work when they grew up.

In the long run, Ney did resume her career; however, looking after children was a priority.

Similarly the MC member Vildan Varol answered with an unqualified "no" before she began recalling that marriage had indeed changed her career patterns. She responsed:

> No, marriage did not change my career. I was already working when I married and my husband knew I was going to work. But actually now that you mention it marriage did curtail my career; as least it shaped it in a certain way. We had to attend an "on the job" training course and I got the highest marks in the course—so I became eligible for this scholarship which would pay for a year's study abroad. On my return I would be promoted to a position in a different branch with better pay and much better advancement opportunities. Well my husband said "no" and that was it.

Most of the women, much like Ney and Varol had to be given time to recall how marriage affected their personal careers. They adapted to the demands of marriage that shaped their careers so thoroughly that the particular reshaping rooted out impressions of an earlier stage. The different ways in which marriage affected personal life plans are summarized in table 21.

Table 21
Changes in Life Plans Due to Marriage

	Female MPs	Male MPs	Female MC Members
No it didn't	4	10	4
Had to quit work for a time	1		
Had to quit work	2		1
Had to leave school	2		3
Had to quit academia and work	1		
Had to look after children	1		1
Curtail advancement in job			1
Not relevant	5		2

The contrast between the responses of male and female politicians in regard to the effects of marriage on their life plans is striking. However, even though marriage meant that they changed their ways more than did men, it did not cripple women, as their election to political office testifies. Women could rely on a support system that relieved them of the responsibilities of the traditional wife/mother role. Those who had children, that is, half of the women interviewed, said that children did not prevent them from doing what they wanted to do in the long run. Maids helped the female MPs look after their children. Mothers and mothers-in-law looked after the children of the MC members. The women politicians could alleviate the pressures of child rearing that normally tie down women who cannot then be employed in the so-called formal sectors of the economy in the metropolitan regions.[15] Those who could not afford a maid relied on their closely-knit traditional family ties, in which neither the parents nor the children are ever absolved of their responsibilities toward each other.

ECONOMIC DECISION MAKING IN THE POLITICIANS' FAMILIES

Female politicians who skillfully adapted to their marital responsibilities had more authority as wives in economic decisions within their families than did the wives of the male politicians or typical Turkish wives. The large majority of the male MPs (9 of 19) said that they decided on economic issues by themselves, even though most of them (6 of 10) qualified their answers and said that they consulted their wives before they decided. As mentioned earlier, in 70 percent of Turkish families the husband decided how the family income was to be spent.[16] Male MPs were in this respect similar to most Turkish husbands. However, female politicians were quite unlike typical Turkish wives. In a society where only about 20 percent of the married couples in nuclear families decide together how to spend the family income, the percentage among female politicians was considerably higher: half the female MPs and more than half the MC members. None of the female politicians said that her husband decided by himself or without consulting her. If the couple did not decide together then the answers were: "I decide by myself" (2 of 12 of the MC members), "I decide by myself, but consult my husband" (2 of 16 of the MPs), "Each decides how to spend his or her money separately" (1 of 16 of the MPs).

The answers become more interesting when we consider that while most of the female MPs were professionals who earned their livelihood, not all the female politicians had independent sources of income. Even though most of the female MC members were housewives, they nevertheless had their say on economic issues. An RPP MC member, Emine Soydam, a housewife married to a military officer, responded to the question on economic decision making in this way.

> There was no such question, i.e., that of who decides on economic issues. There was a family income, my husband happened to bring it home and I was the housewife—but the family income was ours both. He had infinite faith in me, we had mutual faith in each other, I should say. Neither one of us would ask the other how we spent the money or where we spent it. We, neither one of us would misuse it.

Soydam's response was typical of a MC member who had established her authority at home regardless of her pecuniary contribution to the household income. Another example was Ayşe Tar, a JP MC member and a housewife married to a governor. Tar was one of the two MC members who said that she decided on all economic issues herself even though she did not have independent income.

While male MPs decided on economic issues by themselves, the female politicians usually decided with their husbands. Regarding economic decision making, male MPs were similar to most Turkish husbands, whereas female politicians were quite unlike most Turkish wives.

DISCIPLINARY DECISION MAKING IN THE POLITICIANS' FAMILIES

Male MPs who considered themselves to be the patriarchal authorities on economic decisions again mostly said that they had the last word on disciplinary issues in the family (6 of 10). Excluding those who were single, almost all the female politicians (9 of 11 of the MPs, and 8 of 10 of the MC members) said that they shared disciplinary authority with their husbands. In a society where 94 percent of the men and 89 percent of the women in nuclear families think that "men have the last word in the family,"[17] female politicians who thought that they shared authority with men were not only atypical, but also strikingly more assertive. In contrast, male MPs (6 of 10) who considered themselves to have the last word in the family were following accepted norms. Table 22 summarizes the responses to the question of disciplinary authority.

Table 22
Who has the Final Disciplinary Authority at Home

	Female MPs	Male MPs	Female MC Members
Husband	1	6	1
Husband & Wife	9	4	8
Wife	1		1
Not relevant	5		2

Ayşe Nadan, the female MP who said that her husband had the last word in the family explained her answer:

Well we have a patriarchal family at home.[18] I give much respect, too . . ., in fact I am the one who makes him the patriarch. I mean I am the one who makes the family patriarchal. That was what I saw in my family from my father, and I did the same thing to my husband.

This revealing remark indicates how, despite her substantive authority within the family, Nadan feels the need to legitimize it in terms of the patriarchal framework. Ironically, in the process, she asserts her control over the patriarchal arrangement: "I am the one who makes the family patriarchal." We can conclude with considerable certainty that the female politicians have secure authoritative positions in their homes, even though they do not claim a monopoly to it the way men do.[19]

DIVISION OF LABOR

Even though female politicians have more authority in the family than do typical Turkish women, they still take on the typically female household duties. Most of the female politicians (8 of 11 of the MPs, 8 of 10 of the MC members) do not get any help with housework from their husbands, while most male politicians (8 of 10) do not help their wives with the housework. In this case, the female politicians are like the typical housewives—or rather the superwomen—who are housewives as well as career women, while the male politicians are still much like the typical husbands who assume their traditional roles, letting their wives do the housework. The responses on this issue are summarized in table 23.

Table 23
Husband's Help with Housework

	Female MPs	Male MPs	Female MC Members
None	8	8	8
Set table/make salad	2	2	1
Set table/do dishes			1
Shop	1		
Not relevant	5		2

The female politicians who share significant authority with their husbands and yet assume all the housework, do so without any complaints. They offer different explanations, but all the women who do not get any help from their husbands seem to be reconciled to the fact. The RPP MP Ece Can, one of the most outspoken, provocative female politicians with many fans, as well as critics, explains her situation:

My husband never helps with housework. He sometimes, rarely, tries to make a salad or something, but the kitchen becomes a fire site. By God, I do not want him to help me. Someone has to clean up the mess after him.

When it comes to helping in the kitchen, the authority is solely Can's. She decides how the salad should be prepared, and since her husband does not do it to her liking, she does not want him in the kitchen. Because she wants to have her way, she is reconciled to the fact that he does not help with housework.

While Can does not want her husband's help, Gaye Akdan argues that there has never been a need for her husband's help. She explains,

No, he did not help with the housework; but then there was never any need for it, either. I always had help with the housework. As you see even now, I have Hasan wit me.[20]

Akdan still considers herself responsible for housework—the hired help she can afford help perpetuate the functional division of labor between herself and her husband. The question as to whether or not she should expect her husband to help with the housework does not come up.

Finally, one superwoman explains that she is capable and can work both outside and inside the house. The JP MC member Ayşe Tar, a popular politician respected by all, including members of the opposing parties, takes pride in the wide range of her responsibilities. She says,

I do the housework; I am in fact a housewife, but a very capable one. I cook, clean, do the dishes and preside over the organization (Mothers's Association). Rather than go to bridge parties, I help people. I do everything.

Even though Tar's answer suggests that her social and political activities are merely what she does in her spare time, she is a very prominent public figure. All the women politicians accepted their traditional responsibilities, although for differing reasons. Whether they claimed it was because they had the means or the personal stamina, they were fully reconciled to it, without complaint. The confident justifications of these authoritative women implied more of an ability to cope with, rather than a fatalistic acceptance of, their housework responsibilities.

Male MPs responded to the question on whether they did any housework as if it were a rhetorical issue. The typical answer was a curt: "No, my wife does the housework." They were neither apologetic nor eager to talk about it; with matter-of-fact indifference, the response was: "What do you expect." When probed as to whether their wives at times expected them to help or complained about housework, the response was again a simple no, or: "She would not let me do it anyway." While women were ready to justify and explain, men seemed to accept as a matter of course this particular division of labor.

Overview

Perhaps as could be expected, all the politicians interviewed were economically secure, middle class or upper middle class people. Engaging in party politics required some type of financial security. However, what was striking is that the female MPs seemed to be more affluent than their male colleagues. Male MPs, unlike women politicians interviewed, complained at length of the economic problems they had in elections. It is likely that women politicians who had economic problems either could not overcome them to be elected to office, or else they did not have the confidence that they could run for office and overcome the problem. The successful woman politician was economically more priveledged than her male counterpart.

What distinguished the women politicians further was that in their familial life, they were used to sharing power with men. Although all those interviewed came from families where fathers had more authoritative positions than mothers, the woman politicians, unlike the men, thought their fathers shared authority with the mothers. While most women said that their fathers consulted their wives, most men claimed their fathers were the sole decision-makers.

In their present families, the woman politicians, again unlike the men, thought that they shared authority with their spouses. Even though these women assumed the responsibilities of a traditional housewife and structured their lives around their marriages, they had more economic and decision making authority within the family then did typical Turkish women. In terms of familial authority, male MPs were more typical of Turkish men than women politicians were of Turkish women. Unequal sharing of power between men and women was less obtrusive in the families of the women politicians compared to typical Turkish men and women. A pliant patriarchy within the family could be correlated with women's success in the public realm. Women who held politicial office shared men's patriarchal authority in decision making, economic or otherwise.

5
Political Involvement: Male Support and Initiation into Politics

One of the most popular justifications of why women do not hold political office has been that they are not interested in politics. In a patriarchal society where men have always assumed political responsibilities, even if women did not foresee any problems in political participation, we could still expect them to be reticent to participate in politics merely because they do not think of politics as a woman's vocation. In those few cases where women have become politically involved, what then explains their deviating from the norm? Why do they think women should participate in politics? What are the factors that so often inhibit, and yet occasionally motivate, women's political interests and ambitions? In my interviews, I focus on the women's initiation into politics. How does the patriarchal organization of their lives help to facilitate or obstruct women's initiation into politics? Is it political events or personal relations that spark political interest? Do professions politicize? Men and women have significantly different answers.

Should Women be in Politics?

To pursue the question as to why women do not hold political office, I shall first present the normative issue as to why women should participate in politics. Although almost all the politicians interviewed agreed that more women should be in politics, most of the women (9 of 16) who had made it to the Parliament thought that women's gender should not be a justification for women to be in politics: "Yes, there should be more women politicians, but not because they are women." Before they elaborated their reasons as to why women should be in politics, these women parliamentarians explained why women should not be in politics. Oya Fer responded,

"Before anything else, I am strictly opposed to woman's being promoted in politics, if the reason is just that she is a woman. Women are powerful. First they should recognize their own strength"

Affirmative action obviously was not a congenial policy. These women were eager to explain that they neither wanted nor needed "discrimination to be in politics." The fact that many were assuming all the household tasks along with their professional careers and confronting the problems of male discrimination was not an issue.

Other women MPs (5 of 16) thought that women should be in politics because they are women. Female attributes deserved recognition and needed to be promoted. Almost all of the women MCMs (11 of 12) and many of the male MPs (6 of 10) thought likewise. However, there was disagreement as to what constituted these noteworthy female attributes. Most of the women MPs (5 of 7) and MC members (6 of 11) thought that women should participate in politics because they are serious, responsible and hardworking. As mothers, they are used to sacrificing more. MC member Ferhan Noyan explained her reasons:

"I think there should be more women than men in politics. As far as I can see, professional women work harder and more conscientiously than men. Men are always condescending their jobs as if what they are doing is not worthy of them. . . . Also women know so many problems more closely and pursue them better. Men are complaining about inflation, but they don't actually know all that much about it. It is the woman who spends the money and manages the household. Problems of education. . . . Sure, but have you ever seen a father holding his son's hand in front of the school gate. No! It is always the women. We have a saying, "It is the woman who makes a man either a vezier or a scoundrel." Well, it is a very true saying. Let the woman come and do it directly rather than through a man. This is why I think there should be more women in politics."

Noyan's sentiments reflected those of many other women who thought women's gender was a normative justification for more women in politics.

For men who thought likewise, the rhetoric was different. While they agreed that female virtues needed to be promoted, they painted an alternative picture of those virtues. Women were kind and polite and tolerant. They could restrain men and have a positive impact on them. It was not simply that women could improve the quality of political life but that they could be good for men. Yavuz Caka explained,

Women can function as brakes in politics. Because they have maternal compassion, they always prevent reckless acts. It is the way they have been created. Fathers, after all, don't have the compassion and maternal affection women do. And men behave themselves when there are women around.

While Noyan observed that women were hard working, competent and tough, Yavuz Caka claimed that they were soft, temperate, and moderate. Both drew on woman's capacity for motherhood, but they associated maternity with different merits. Yavuz Caka's more stereotypical perception of women as kind and supportive contrasted with Noyan's view of women who could competently manage their family and society. Yes, the women should be in politics, but the women politicians thought it was because women were strong whereas the men said it was because the women were soft.

POLITICAL INVOLVEMENT: THE ALTERNATIVE PATHS

Male and female politicians who believed that women should be in politics for different reasons moved into the political realm through distinctly different paths. While men were mostly politicized in response to major political events, women became politically involved through personal relations. The politicization process of male and females sharply distinguished them from each other.

MALE MPS AND POLITICAL EVENTS

The responses to the question, "Can you recall and/or specify the most significant event in your initiation into politics (i.e., active political involvement)?" revealed the striking difference in the initiation patterns of male and female politicians. For the woman politician, there was "nothing in particular" (6 of 16 MPs, 5 of 12 MCMs) or she was merely "recruited" (2 of 16 MPs), she slowly moved in through social work, (4 of 12 MCMs) or it was all a coincidence (1 of 16 MPs, 1 of 12 MCMs). Only a few (4 of 16 MPs, 2 of 12 MCMs) claimed that political events politicized them. For the male MPs, on the contrary, political events were crucial in political involvement (9 of 20).

Most of the male MPs came from apolitical families and decided to participate in politics during their university years or soon after they graduated. The RPP-DP rivalry between 1945 and 1960 was the most powerful politicizing event for these men (Orhan Il, Osman Dur, Yavuz Caka, Ismail Or, Osman Nuri, Latif Arif Sarı). Emergence of the DP meant that they had to protect the Kemalist party and register as RPP members or challenge the RPP monopoly of power and support the DP. İsmail Or's response was typical of the RPP representatives. He explained,

> In the '50s when we were studying in law school, we were drawn into a whirlpool of politics. It was a struggle of the Kemalist forces in the society. We were the Atatürk children broght up to uphold the Kemalist principles. I registered RPP and worked in an ocak when I was still a student living in the student dorms in Beyazıt.[1] It was a question of self respect.

İsmail Or's personal involvement with the political developments that were taking place in the country in the 1950's marked his initiation into politics. Defending the RPP was defending oneself and those principles one was educated to respect. With the possible exception of one, all the RPP men strongly believed in the RPP principles at least when they registered.

The JP MPs who registered with the DP resented the RPP monopoly of power. They had no particular urge to uphold the Kemalist principles. They witnessed the RPP create a massive bureaucracy, neglect the provinces, tax the rich and the poor. Registering with the DP was an effort to curb the power of the RPP. Yavuz Caka, who registered JP when he graduated from law school, explains,

> We are from Rize. For the past 20 years that the RPP ruled the country, the so-called Rize MP did not deign visit Rize let alone find out what our problems were. We just paid taxes to the state and did not get anything anything back. We had enough of the RPP. I wanted to register DP.

Whether the RPP rule was actually oppressive or the DP challenge anti-Kemalist, the male MPs were deeply interested in the political developments of their time. They decided to become politically involved, usually along with friends who shared the political fervor of the day.

A slightly different group of men were those who were politicized in their professions. Like the other male MPs, the men in this group (Osman Kaş, Uğur Er, Galip Far, Ahmet Hikmet Başar) came from apolitical families where there was no question of family members inspiring their political interests. However, unlike the others who were politicized in response to a political upheaval that had a nationwide impact, these men responded to political issues that developed in the course of their professional careers.

For example, Osman Kaş, a cab driver who registered RPP during the single party era, explained that his professional career necessitated his political involvement. At the time, he was only a member of the Cab Drivers' Association, of which he later became the president. He argued that, "One could not get anywhere (among the drivers) unless one belonged to the party." Having political connections increased one's status and chances of promotion within the Drivers' Association.

On the other hand, Ahmet Hikmet Başar was a renowned judge who frequently published articles in the left-of-center newspaper *Cumhuriyet*. He resented the political harassment of the JP sympathizers who accused him of pro-RPP verdicts, and resigned to air his beliefs in the political arena. He registered with the RPP.

Uğur Er received his law degree and began to work in a labor union. His advocacy of the labor unions committed Er to a political stance typically represented by the RPP. Even though he did not register RPP, Er was already a highly politicized man, actively propagating his political ideas through his professional commitments. Eventually RPP recognized him as a political asset and persuaded him to join.

WOMEN POLITICIANS AND PERSONAL RELATIONS

Unlike the male MPs, the woman politicians were politicized more in response to the influence of relatives rather than political events. The familial encouragement they received sharply distinguished male from female politicians with regard to their entry into politics. Slightly more than half of the female MPs (9 of 16), half the MC members and about two-fifths (4 of 10) of the male MPs had close relatives in politics.

Table 24
Family Members in Politics

	Female MPs	Male MPs	Female MC Members
Father	4	1	3
Husband	3		2
Brother	2	1	
Father-in-law		1	
Uncle		1	
Mother			1
Total in Politics	9	4	6
Total interviewed	16	10	12

Most of the politically involved relatives of the female politicians (8 of 9 of the female MPs and 3 of 6 of the MC members) were MPs or leading party figures. The male MPs were related to politicians with lower status, such as party members at district organizations. In other words, female politicians had closer relatives (i.e., husbands and fathers, rather than in-laws and uncles) with higher political status than the male MPs.

At home, the female politicians considered their parents, especially their fathers, to be more politically inclined than did the male politicians. While many women (7 of 16 of the MPs, and 5 of 12 of the MC members) said that their fathers had definite political interests, only one male MP out of ten thought likewise. There were no women MPs who said that their fathers were apolitical, while some male MPs (3 of 10) and MC members (3 of 12) considered their fathers to be apolitical. As for the mothers, with the exception of one, all the male MPs (9 of 10), more than half the female MPs (10 of 16) and some of the MC members (4 of 12) said that their mothers were apolitical. The mothers of female politicians, especially the mothers of the MC members, seemed to be more political than the mothers of the male politicians. In the homes of female politicians where the fathers had significant political interest, even though the mothers might have only been affected by their husbands, the fact remains that in relation to the male politicians, the female politicians thought they had parents who were more politically interested. Table 25 shows the politicians' responses to the question concerning their parents' political dispositions.

Accordingly, when asked to evaluate the political atmosphere in the parents' home, more female politicians said there was a political atmosphere in their parents' home than did the male politicians. About half the male MPs said that there was no political atmosphere at home; in contrast, none of the female MPs and only a few of the MC members (3 of 12) gave the same answer. Table 26 summarizes their answers.

The female politicians came from families where politics was part of the private family life. Their parents, especially their fathers, even when they were not actively involved, were nevertheless interested in politics. In contrast, male politicians had neither many political relatives nor were they brought up in households with a significant political atmosphere. Their fathers, unlike those of the female politicians, were not particularly interested in politics.

In view of the preponderance of politically interested family members in the families of the female politicians, it is not surprising that they received strong encouragement to become politically involved. Half the female MPs and half the MC members, unlike the

Table 25
Political Disposition of Parents

	Father's Political Disposition			Mother's Political Disposition		
	Female MPs	Male MPs	MC Members	Female MPs	Male MPs	MC Members
Political interests	7	1	5			3
Follow politics, but not involved	5	2	1	1		
Follow news but not political	3	2	1	4	1	1
Patriotic	1	2	2	1		4
Apolitical		3	3	10	9	4
TOTAL	16	10	12	16	10	12

Table 26
Political Atmosphere at Home

	Female MPs	Male MPs	MC Members
Political atmosphere	5		3
Follow politics but not involved	5	1	3
Follow news but not necessarily political	6	4	3
Apolitical atmosphere		5	3
TOTAL	16	10	12

male MPs, said that either their fathers or their husbands sparked their interest, urging them to be politically involved or giving active support to their nascent interests. The male politicians (9 of 10) who did not have the active encouragement of their close family members had friends who supported them. However, this support derived more from a sense of comradeship rather than positive encouragement. Table 27 summarizes their responses.

Table 27
Personal Relations who Encouraged Politicization

	Female MPs	Male MPs	MC Members
Father	5	1	2
Wife/Husband	3		5
Friend	3	9	3
Mother			1
None	5		1
TOTAL	16	10	12

Personal relations could have affected these politicians, not merely by encouraging them but also by discouraging them. However, all the MC members, a majority of the female MPs and most of the male MPs said that their relatives and friends did not discourage them from politics. The responses to the question are summarized in table 28.

Table 28
Personal Relations Who Discouraged Political Involvement

	Female MPs	Male MPs	MC Members
Father		3	
Wife/Husband	1		
Friend			
Mother	1		
None	14	7	12
TOTAL	16	10	12

Neither male nor female politicians had much opposition from their relatives or friends as they got involved in politics. Contrary to what might have been expected in a patriarchal society where men have traditionally monopolized political office, the few women who were elected to office had significant personal support from the patriarchs in their families. In encouraging these women to be politically involved, the fathers and brothers were devolving political authority to women within the constraints of a patriarchal society.

Women Politicians and the Alternative Paths of Political Involvement

While personal influences were clearly the most prominent aspect of women politicians' politicization process, we can nevertheless distinguish different patterns of their entry into politics. Men, as fathers and husbands, shaped women's political lives differently than men who recruited them into politics. Women, on the other hand, responded to political influences at various stages of their lives and acted upon such influences differently. We can differentiate five alternative patterns of women's initiation into politics.

MALE RELATIVES AS ROLE MODELS

The political interests of the women in this group (the MPs Banu Ay, Beyhan Sunar, Tülin Sağlam, Kısmet Zarif and the MCMs

Sevim Han, Olcay Fen, Ayşe Tar, and Taylan Mor) were sparked by their close male relatives, in most cases their fathers, and sometimes their husbands. These women were genuinely interested in politics when they decided to register in their respective political parties; they were not recruited into politics and often no one persuaded them to get politically involved immediately prior to their registration. The women who had been influenced by their fathers looked up to these men. Typically, the daughters responded to the political atmosphere at home created by their fathers and internalized the father's political convictions, later promoting these beliefs on their own.

The case of Banu Ay is an example. Ay was a young senator respected by her colleagues; she worked through the party ranks to rise quickly to the top as the president of the Istanbul RPP Women's Branch before being elected to the Senate. Ay remembered her father, a high-level civil servant, as "deeply involved in and deeply affected by politics." She said that during the DP years when he worked in the civil service, all bureaucrats were immersed in politics since politicians appointed bureaucrats at their own discretion for political reasons. Banu Ay proudly explained that she came from a family in which politics has been a family tradition since her grandfather, who was a Young Turk. Even though she was interested in social and political problems from her teenage days, "reading political journals when girls her age read love stories," no one ever told Ay that she should consider getting politically involved. After she finished law school and began working as an independent lawyer, she decided to register with the RPP. As she put it, political life was her ideal and politics would fill her life. Her father died when she was still in school and her mother did not approve of her political interests, however, Ay always believed that had her father been alive he would have given her his full support.

For some other women politicians, the impact of the father's political involvement was more direct. The fathers were either active politicians or they encouraged the daughters more directly. The MCM Olcay Fen thought of political involvement only after her politician father was arrested in the 1960 coup. Fen's father was a DP MP. Even though there was no one who encouraged her to participate actively in politics, she developed her political interests in the family. She lived through the RPP era in the home of a DP MP who was later banned from politics in a pro-RPP coup. Though no one knew of her intention to register JP, after doing so, the first thing she did was to inform her father, who approved.

In the case of Tülin Sağlam, she reacted to conservative DP

policies: Sağlam resented that the call to prayer was read in Arabic, a policy promoted by the DP to appease the party's religious constituency. Yet, it was Sağlam's father who had until then cultivated her political interests and who, in fact, channeled her resentment into political engagement. He earnestly advocated that she register RPP and work in the party.

In other cases, the husband, rather than the father, was the patriarchal figure who cultivated the women politicians' political interest. Both the MP Kısmet Zarif and the MCM Ayşe Tar were wives of politicians. Even though the husbands did not explicitly urge their wives to become politically involved, these women developed their political interests via their husbands. Both Zarif and Tar became involved in their husband's political work and were themselves in politics before their husbands left politics. For women in this group, initiation into politics was a private matter that took shape within the patriarchal family, bound by the patriarchal tie.

THE HUSBAND'S WIFE OR THE FATHER'S DAUGHTER

The women in this group (the MPs Ayşe Nadan and Gül Narcı) cultivated their political interests after they were recruited to their parties. One of the two women in this group was the daughter of a distinguished political figure while the other was the wife of a prominent MP. After the 1960 coup, both of these popular DP politicians were banned from politics. The JP, which replaced the DP after the coup, promptly asked these women to contest the elections in those provinces where the ex-DP politicians still had their strong constituencies. By trying to establish their political strength, the party leaders inadvertently spurred the political careers of these women. In turn, these women had a personal stake in maintaining their family names in politics. Gül Narcı, whose father was one of the architects of the multiparty era, was deeply distressed witnessing her father's descent from power and the endless accusations made against her family. She resolved to redress these perceived injustices of the coup when her youngest daughter was taught in elementary school to condemn her grandfather because he was a DP member. Ayşe Nadan found herself similarly harassed. She belonged to a family of leading politicians, both on her father's and on her husband's side. After the coup, she considered herself and her family "unjustifiably denounced." Both these women felt personally slandered in the political climate of the post-1960 era; when the JP politicians asked them to become candidates, both accepted the offer without much hesitation. Personal resentment stemming from a political event was channelled into political involvement. Had it not been for the leaders' political calculations, it is likely that these women would not have engaged in politics by themselves, no matter how much they resented the coup.

The women who were recruited by party members were not always recruited to carry on their fathers' name. A number of women who were initiated into politics by close male relatives, mostly fathers, brothers or husbands (among the MPs: Emel Uğur, Ece Can, Dilek Ser, Gaye Akdan, and Nergis Ney; among the MCMs: Mahper Yık, Handan Yavaş, and Huriye Maslak) would not have embarked upon political careers had it not been for party members who successfully recruited them. It was not only women from Woman's Branches but rather men from the main cadres that recruited many women who then became committed politicians.

Among the MPs Ece Can was a typical example of a recruited woman with political interests sparked by a patriarchal figure. Can was a colorful MP who secured her seat after years of party work. Many praised her self-confident, outspoken manner, while others— mainly her male colleagues—accused her of lacking in tact. Nevertheless, she was a politician none could afford to ignore. Like most other female MPs, Can was initiated into politics by her father, a committed RPP sympathizer who was harrassed for advocating RPP politics in the DP president's home town. She went along with him to political campaigns, witnessed how he was ostracized by DP sympathizers in a DP town, and lived through the hard times that this entailed for the family.[2] During her university years, as the daughter of a staunch RPP advocate, she worked in some pro-RPP student organizations. But after she left law school to marry the son of a provincial landowner, she became a traditional Turkish housewife, dutifully obeying her in-laws, bearing children, even doing menial jobs she had never done before to avoid conflict with her husband's parents. As the educated, city bride in the province, she was a prominent figure well liked by the townswomen. When the RPP Woman's Branch came to Çatalca to organize a district branch, they met Can, who was by then a socially active member in the community of Çatalca women. The Woman's Branch recognized Can's energy and drive and recruited her into the RPP ranks. Can, who had a new-born daughter and a traditional family to deal with, first hesitated to assume an active role in the Çatalca organization—

her daughter had to grow older and she had to have more autonomy within her family, before she could assume a responsible position within the party. However, when the WB in Çatalca elected her as its president in her absence, she gave in. Can's active political career, in which she became one of the first female MC presidents before she was elected an MP, thus began with party recruitment.

Women recruited to politics by other women were few in number (besides Ece Can, there was only Emel Uğur). Many were recruited by male relatives, male friends or male party members. Among the MCMs recruited into politics by men, Mahper Yık was elected to office for three consecutive years until she decided not to run again. Narrating how she became politically involved, Yık remembered her father as a political man who had taken an active part in the Kemalist movement; while she was growing up, the house would be full of her father's friends coming and going, talking of politics. At the university Yık studied literature and became a teacher. Although she enjoyed teaching literature, after she had a child, she left her job, and divorced soon after. She had not thought of active political participation until her male friends, who recognized her public concerns, urged her to register RPP. Yık did not resist. A public occupation would give meaning to her life that the new job she had did not. She was brought up to uphold public values as the daughter of a Kemalist patriot and responded favorably to being recruited into public life.

At times, relatives rather than friends recruited women into politics. Handan Yavaş an outspoken MC member who intimidated many of her colleagues with her sharp criticisms, became involved in politics because of her brother. Yavaş's brother, who was a RPP member, insisted on registering his sister in the RPP and eventually did so. Had it not been for him, Yavaş would not have had the initiative to get involved politically.

It is very likely that the women in this category would not have been in politics had they not been recruited by their respective parties. Yet had they not been exposed to politics earlier through male relatives, it is very likely that these women would not have responded to party recruitment or attracted the party members' attention. At the time they were recruited into politics, most could not say, "a political life was my ideal" as Banu Ay had said when she went and registered in her party; however, once they were given the opportunity and encouragement, the women in this category, no less than those who registered on their own, committed themselves to politics, and eventually assumed political offices.

RECRUITMENT OF THE APOLITICAL WOMEN

Women recruited to politics were not always women interested in politics; among the female politicians in my sample, there were apolitical women (among the MPs: Kerime Sahip, Cemile Ay, and Ezel Nur Pars, and the MCMs Belkıs Nil and Figen Naz) who were recruited to office or to the party ranks because they were socially active or professionally recognized women from whose membership the party would benefit. For example, the DP MP Ezel Nur Pars, elected for two consecutive terms to office, was an associate professor interested in geology when the campaigning DP president met her. Ezel Nur Pars had neither any political relatives nor any interest in politics until she was offered candidacy in the parliamentary elections. Confronted with bureaucratic problems in the university that delayed her tenure, she decided to go into politics as a temporary solution to her academic problems. Similarly the DP MP Cemile Ay and the RPP MP Kerime Sahip were publicly recognized professional women. Neither of them came from a political family. Even though Sahip, an economist in the State Planning Agency, had supervised a project for the RPP Research Center, she had no interest in active political participation let alone a seat in the National Assembly until the RPP leaders approached to nominate her in the parliamentary elections.

Among the MCMs, both Belkıs Nil and Figen Naz were apolitical women, socially active in their respective communities. Popular as they were, they had no interest in political involvement, no previous political experience, and no political connections. They were recruited to their respective political parties by friends of some friends who noticed their successful social activism and urged them to become politically involved. Both Nil and Naz registered in their respective parties more for the sake of friends than their own interest in politics, but later became members of the MC.

In this category the initiation of women into politics was coincidental. Only when they were in politics did they develop political interests to become active members of the political rather than a social community. Had they not been recruited, they would not have had the opportunity to convert their social activism into political activism. Following their political recruitment, they assumed positions of leadership within the party, held political seats and at times were reelected to office.

WOMEN WITHOUT THE MEN

Finally, a small group of women (the MPs İkbal Ful Hak and Oya

Fer, and the MCMs Ferhan Noyan, Emine Soydam, and Vildan Varol) who decided to go into politics on their own, without any patriarchal influence or party recruitment. Like male MPs, these women responded to political events. However, the events that these women responded to were limited in scope and of a more personal nature. Two of the five women in this group—one an MP, the other an MCM—were members of the Turkish Labor Party, articulate committed politicians who were exposed to socialist ideology in their university years. The political impact of the Labor Party and the socialist ideology was limited in scope within the formal framework of Turkish politics. While in no way divorced from their families, these women did not have any active support from their families when they decided to become members of the Labor Party. Registering TLP was a matter of political conviction which did not concern their families.

Besides the two socialist women, others were politicized outside the family framework in response to political/social events. For example, Emine Soydam decided to be politically involved when she witnessed the plight of Anatolian women. While she traveled in Anatolia in military posts along with her husband, Soydam felt that she should help these deprived women. When the RPP WB came to a town they were in to organize a local branch, she registered RPP.

Another example of a female politician who decided to become politically involved without any political connections is Vildan Varol. Varol, "an Atatürk child," as she calls herself, decided to go into politics following her early retirement from an insurance company. Except for its lucrative aspects, she was not satisfied with her job and believed that politics would provide the opportunity for public service that would also give her personal satisfaction. Given her admiration for the Kemalist principles that had directly shaped the RPP program, she registered RPP. In Varol's case, Kemalist public education instilled in her the respect for the good of the country, as well as inclining her towards the principles of the RPP.

The women who decided to engage in politics on their own without the inspiration or the actual encouragement of any male relative were perhaps closest to the male politicians in the way they became politically involved.

Overview

Political events or personal relations were, in the case of the politicians interviewed, the two alternative factors which critically shaped political involvement. Whereas most male MPs were politiziced in response to political events that had a nationwide impact, most of the women responded to the influence of the political men in their lives. As fathers and husbands, men sparked women's political interests, and as male politicians they recruited women into politics. Unlike women, male MPs decided to become politically involved along with friends who shared similar convictions.

Among the women politicians, the role of close male relatives in initiating women into politics was lesser in the case of the MCMs than among of the MPs. Unlike the female MPs, there were no MC members, for example, who capitalized on the name of their father or husband in the elections. Furthermore, more MCMs came from apolitical families and decided to go into politics on their own. Yet, the rule remained that women's initiation into politics became possible and, hence, constrained within the bonds of a patriarchal relationship. Without the authoritative male backing, only a few women could move into politics. The tradition of men exercising political power defined the parameters within which women exercised political power.

6
Getting Elected

There is a Turkish proverb that "The watermill does not turn with water carried to it" (Taşıma suyla değirmen dönmez). A natural flow is needed to propel the mill. Women initiated and recruited into politics by men have, as it were, propelled the political mill with the water they carried to it. A political aspirant typically intends to be elected to office and follows the paths of recruitment, shaping a political career around this goal.[1] Yet the women interviewed neither planned a career in elective office in advance of their nomination nor cultivated the political networks necessary for nomination to office. Moving into politics was not enough to get elected to office. What were the opportunities and obstacles that facilitated or hindered women's access to political office?

Will to Get Elected to Office

Women politicians viewed their election to office more like a promotion in the party ranks than the realization of a career goal. When questioned as to why they wanted to hold office, most women politicians (8 of 16 of the MPs, 9 of 12 of the MCMs) said that it was not because they wanted or intended to hold office, but rather because they were expected to do so. The woman MP Beyhan Sunar explained,

> I did not have the slightest idea of wanting to become an MP. I was a committed RPP member working for the party; but once you are in it, you can't leave it. Circumstances shape what you should become or else you leave everything and go back to your profession.[2]

Similarly the parliamentarian Banu Ay said that it was the party administration that insisted that she be a candidate in the city council election. After her term in the city council, she was asked to preside over the Woman's Branch of her party. Finally her colleagues pushed her, nominating her for parliament. In fact these women were proud that they did not pursue the goal of holding office. Such a pursuit would have been immodest. The MCM Belkıs Nil explained,

> My friends promoted me. Everything happened with their push. I never nominate myself anyway. It was not in my mind in the first place. I can proudly say that I never worked to be elected.

Not working to be elected was for Nil an occasion for self-compliment. Similarly, Figen Naz, who had very strong chances of being elected had she run for office, preferred to be appointed rather than elected to the MC. When the secretary general of the party asked her if she would like to be an appointed member she agreed. She put it: "To be honest, I considered this offer coming from such an important person a great honor." The implication is that running for office would be less honorable.

Among the male MPs there were also those (5 of 10) who thought election to the parliament was a promotion through the party ranks rather than a career goal to be actively pursued. Uğur Er made the same point as many women when he said:

> It is not a question of "wanting" though of course becoming an MP is an ego boost. It is a natural promotion, once you become involved in politics.

However, the male politicians did not need the encouragement and support women needed to run for office. Most of their wives (7 of 10) discouraged them for running for office but they competed for office and succeeded anyway. The disapproval of their wives was of little consequence. When they felt they had established themselves in the party ranks, they could not be easily be dissuaded from participating in the elections.

Career Lines

Regardless of what their career goal was, both men and women worked in the party ranks before they held elective office. In the metropolitan areas, those who had the right educational and professional credentials usually followed the route through party cadres to parliament.[3] We can see at work here what R.K. Merton has called a "status sequence" to the top: political aspirants moved from positions of low status to high status through the party ranks developing the informal networks which facilitated claims to candidacy.[4] The typical male MP worked in the main party cadres, usually at the district (ilçe) or the provincial (il) level, to be elected to the municipality council, or at times to the provincial council.

A typical RPP MP, Osman Nuri registered in the Ankara Demirtepe ocak in 1957. He worked in the ocak administrative council before he settled in Istanbul. There he began working in the Üsküdar RPP District Administrative Council; he was then elected first to the RPP Istanbul Provincial Advisory Council and to the RPP Istanbul Provincial Disciplinary Commission. In 1968, he was elected to the Istanbul Provincial Council (İl Meclisi) as the RPP representative. In 1973 he became an MP.

Similarly, Yavuz Caka, a typical JP MP, joined the DP ranks in 1945 after he graduated from law school. He worked to set up the Beykoz DP organization. He became the president of the DP Anadolu Hisarı division (bucak), then worked as a member of the Beykoz District Administrative Council before he was elected to the Istanbul MC for two consecutive terms between 1950 and 1960. Meanwhile he became the vice president of the DP Istanbul Provincial Administrative Council. In 1974 he was elected to Parliament. At least in the metropolitan areas, the male MPs were no newcomers either to politics or to their parties.

Table 29 summarizes how the politicians interviewed came to assume their political office. As indicated above, both male (8 of 10) and female politicians (12 of 16 of the MPs, 10 of 12 of the MCMs) worked in the party cadres before they assumed political office. Among the women politicians appointed to parliament without prior party work, two of the MPs were representatives before 1960 when channels for political recruitment were not clearly established. The two other women, appointed after 1960, were close relatives of prominent DP politicians drawing votes from the DP sympathizers. Among the MCMs, one prominent professional was appointed to office by party leaders. Among the men, a labor union lawyer and a well-known pro-RPP judge did not work in the party cadres before holding office.

LENGTH OF PARTY WORK

Even though both male and female MPs worked in the party ranks, women politicians had been in politics for a shorter period at the time they were elected to office. Male MPs, who were all elected to Parliament after 1960, had been politically active since the 1950's. There were only two exceptions. Among the twelve female MPs

Table 29
Routes to Political Office

	Female MPs	Male MPs	Female MC Members
Prior Party Work before Election to Office	12	8	10
Nature of the party work through party cadres:			
Provincial Council	2	2	1
Municipality Council	5	4	
Youth Branch exclusively		1	
Woman's Branch exclusively			5
Work in party cadres yet appointed to office	3		2
Party work outside party cadres before appointment to office	2	1	2
Recruited to party as a prospective candidate		1	1
"Big name" elected to office		1	
Appointment without prior party work	4		1
Total interviewed	16	10	12

elected after 1960, only four—Tülin Sağlam, Ece Can, Beyhan Sunar, and Oya Fer—began their political careers in the 1950s. Those who participated in the DP-RPP disputes (4 of 16) were all elected prior to 1960. Among the female MC members who were all elected post-1960, again only four (4 of 12) began their party work before 1960.

Woman's Branches

Even though most women were expected to participate in politics through Woman's Branches, all the women elected to parliament worked in the main party organization for at least one stage in their careers. Only among the MCMs were there women who worked only in Woman's Branches. While the party structure encouraged women to participate in politics through Woman's Branches, channels to the top required going through the main party organization.[5] Those women who were fit to compete with men in the main party organizations were deemed eligible for election to the Parliament. Women had to recognize the limitations of Woman's Branches regarding election to higher office and take the initiative to rise to the top within the main party ranks.

At every level of party organization, promotion of a woman politician meant moving from a Woman's Branch to the main organization regardless of how high her status was in the Woman's Branch. For example, Tülin Sağlam began her political career at the ocak/bucak (subdistrict) level where there were no Woman's Branches, then worked in the Ilçe (district) Woman's Branch, became its president, and switched to the main organization to become only a member at the ilçe level. She was elected to the Istanbul Provincial Council as an RPP representative and then became the president of an RPP ilçe organization at the main level before her election to the parliament. Only after she was elected to the Istanbul Provincial Council did she become eligible to preside over a main ilçe organization, even though she had presided over a Woman's Branch ilçe organization much earlier in her career. Similarly, Oya Fer became a member of the main party after she served as the vice president of the Woman's Branches at the higher provincial level. Fer had registered at an ocak, worked as an ocak and later bucak president, became the vice president of the Provincial Woman's Branch at the bucak level, then the president of a Woman's Branch at the ilçe level, before she served in the main organization as a member of the ilçe Administrative Council. She was the president of the Provincial Woman's Branch prior to her election to the Parliament. The Woman's Branch hierarchy was always considered lower in rank to that of the main organization.

Among the politicians interviewed, many men (5 of 10) and women (7 of 16 of the MPs, 4 of 12 of the MCMs) were either "against" Woman's Branches or "both for and against" them (5 of 16 of the female MPs, 5 of 12 of the MCMs, and 2 of 10 of the male MPs). However when they explained that they thought of these institutions, only a few brought up the role of Woman's Branches in the promotion of women. Most women who were against Woman's Branches pointed out that these institutions curtailed their contact with the main organization (9 of 16 of the female MPs, 3 of 12 of the MCMs, 2 of 10 of the male MPs) and subordinated them to men (3 of 16 of the female MPs, 8 of 12 of the MCMs, and 3 of 10 of the men). Beyhan Sunar, a woman MP who was the head of the Provincial Woman's Branch before she was elected to parliament explained:

Well, Woman's Branches help women go into politics. Men control politics, and it is difficult for women to come near politics; but I have to underline, things being as they are, Woman's Branches are ploys of men. Women do not have the authority to stand up for themselves. The district presidents (of the main organization) pressure women into obedience, or else they (the main party presidents) use their clout within the party to have women who will obey them elected to important posts in Woman's Branches. Those elected are somehow always women amenable to men. . . . There is an incredible pressure on women when they are organized in a different organization.

Sunar recognizes that Woman's Branches make politics accessible to women; however, she also argues that these organizations help to establish male politicians' institutional control over women. When women work together in Woman's Branches, male leaders who easily coopt the women leaders extend their control over women in politics.

Men who were against these institutions said that Woman's Branches were socially and politically ineffective organizations (5 of 10 of the male MPs, 1 of 16 of the female MPs, none of the MCMs). The male MP Orhan Il, like a number of his colleagues, spoke vehemently against the Woman's Branches:

Woman's Branches are like idle social organizations. What happens— they drink tea and coffee and gossip. If women were assimilated into the party and worked in the main organization, they would be more successful. They would then be working like comrades. Main organization is the real thing in politics. There lies the key. The cliques are formed in the main party cadres, the primary lists are arranged there. If it is politics at the local levels, again the district politics (of the main party organization) is the main thing. If I am the president of the district organization, and if the Woman's Branch in my district does not follow my line, I will make sure to bring a different woman. Of course, the party bosses might support them, but these women cannot stand on their own by themselves.

Il believes that Woman's Branches are ineffective organizations manipulated by party leaders. As a former party leader who had much clout within the party organization, Il ironically agrees with most of the female politicians who are against Woman's Branches because, they feel, the party leaders exploit these institutions. Condescending as he is, Il sustains the women politicians' accusations that men manipulate women in politics. With radically different normative stands, both men and women who argue against Woman's Branches testify to the fact that Woman's Branches are manipulated by male politicians.

Only a few (3 of 16 of the female MPs, 1 of 12 of the MCMs, 2 of 10 of the male MPs) supported these institutions without reservation. Women speaking in favor of Woman's Branches argued that these institutions made politics accessible to women who would otherwise shy away, from political involvement (6 of 16 of the female MPs, 5 of 12 of the MCMs, 1 of 10 of the male MPs). Some men (2 of 10) pointed out that Woman's Branches promoted party ideology among women, that is, it was good for the party. Two women MPs, a woman MCM and a male MP said that these institutions helped women rise through the party ranks. Nergis Ney, who like most female politicians, embarked on her political career through the Woman's Branches, explained herself in these words:

> I think of the Woman's Branches as a council. It is organized to educate women. The woman who has never been in politics before will be intimidated working shoulder to shoulder with men in the main organization. But if you bring her up from the Woman's Branches then they can adapt. Like me, then I worked in the main organization. They [Woman's Branches] are useful if properly instituted and if they function properly.

Ney believes Woman's Branches can prepare the uninitiated woman to engage in politics along with men. She assumes that women will move up from the Woman's Branches into the main cadres. When probed whether it might be more difficult for women working among women to move into the main cadres, Ney said, "Perhaps, but not necessarily. I am an example. And also, what if they don't? It is not a law that everyone should be in the main cadres." When the question of women's promotions through the main party organizations to improve their chances of candidacy is not a central issue, as is the case for Ney, Woman's Branches can be justified more easily.

Political Network

Working in the party ranks was perhaps a necessary, but clearly not a sufficient condition for election to parliament. Political aspirants who worked in their respective parties needed political cliques that would support their candidacy in the primary elections. To be elected to the municipality council, one could lead a successful campaign without collaborating with other candidates. At the local level, delegates were fewer in number. One could reach them more easily and gain their support. At the parliamentary level however one needed a larger network and an effective collaboration with other candidates. Most of the male politicians (8 of 10) were elected to Parliament as members of small cliques. Four to eight people who belonged to the same faction within the party formed a clique. They then coordinated their campaign activities, each asking their own constituents among the delegates to vote for the clique as a group. Electoral success depended on the successful cooperation of a clique.

Among the women MPs elected after 1960, only Tülin Sağlam, Ece Can, Banu Ay, and Beyhan Sunar (4 of 12) were assisted into office by cliques with male members. Oya Fer, who had long years of service in the party and the municipality council, was elected to office more because of the unusual lobbying of the Provincial Woman's Branch over which she presided than because of any party clique to which she belonged. Ney became an MP (in her first nomination to office) because the proportional representation system then adapted (Milli Bakiye) allowed the party to appoint another MP. There was a consensus among the party leaders that she be named. In her second election, she campaigned on her own. İkbal Ful Hak was the representative of the Labor Party, which had difficulty finding candidates let along having enough candidates to form cliques. Dilek Ser was again a candidate from a small party New Turkey Party, elected from a small province that could have only three representatives. The other four representatives—Ayşe Nadan, Gül Nara, Kerime Sahip, and Kısmet Zarif—were all placed on the primary list from above.

Among those who held office prior to 1960, Emel Uğur, one of the first women to actively participate in politics after the single-party era, worked for a long time in the main party organization and tried to get elected to Parliament, yet could not. She was elected head of the RPP Central Woman's Branch, presided over an important ilçe organization of the main party in the capital, was elected a member of the Provincial Administrative Council again in the main RPP organization in Ankara—and still could not succeed in being elected to Parliament in her first two attempts. Uğur indeed had a record of committed party work. She worked to organize the first Woman's Branches in Turkey, became a successful head of a large (main cadre) district organization and an articulate member of the Administrative Council: however the route to parliamentary office was not merely through successful party work but also required support from the right cliques. When she finally became an MP it was by appointment. Kısmet Zarif, appointed after 1960, was similarly a prominent party member; she was the first woman elected to the Party Council, the highest decision making organ within the party hierarchy. Like Uğur, she had worked extensively starting and organizing Woman's Branches throughout Anatolia; yet she did not have the powerful cliques supporting her candidacy in the primary elections.

Overview

The typical MP from a metropolitan area had to work his or her way up through the party cadres, become established within the party organization and form the right political clique with other candidates to secure nomination for a parliamentary seat. Most of the men interviewed secured their election to parliament as such.

For the woman politician, the route to Parliament was more uneven. The few women who served in the Parliament followed disparate paths to their parliamentary seats. Because the women in politics were expected to work in the Woman's Branches of their parties rather than in the main party organization, moving up through the party ranks was a more circuitous process for the women than the men. Only those who could become accepted in the main organization had any chance of election. Hence, the women working in Woman's Branches had to switch to the main cadres to acquire the necessary status and skills for candidacy.

Yet working up through the party hierarchy was not enough. Women who had moved up within the party organization could not establish the political cliques that would support their candidacy in the elections. Many were appointed rather than elected to office. Others made populist appeals on their own rather than work with a clique. Being elected to office required skills other than those necessary to be a commited party worker. Even though the Woman's Branches appeared to give women the opportunity to commit themselves to politics, to hold political office women had to extricate themselves from these organizations and learn to play by men's rules in the main organization. Established institutions thus constrained women's access to political office.

7
Obstacles to Election: Limits to Male Support?

Above and beyond institutional setbacks, it is common knowledge that women confront numerous other problems in their attempts to rise to the top through political channels. Their traditional roles hinder their public activities.[1] They cannot raise the funds necessary for election campaigns.[2] The electorate is often sceptical of them.[3] Allegations of sexual impropriety undermine their legitimacy.[4] Men discriminate against them often unintentionally and, occasionally, quite intentionally.[5]

Do Turkish women in politics confront similar challenges? In the previous chapters, we saw that the rules of the political game worked against women in getting elected. Beyond these, what are the perceived difficulties that beset Turkish women's political aspirations within traditional political institutions? In the Turkish case, fathers and husbands inspired or encouraged women to get politically involved. Many women were recruited into politics by men. Did this male support continue in politics?

A Smooth Election to Office?

When asked what, if any, problems they had in getting elected, both male and female politicians said that they did not have major problems. Most of the women (11 of 16 of the MPs and 11 of 12 of the MCMs) and more than half of the male MPs (6 of 10) were elected to office at their first candidacy. As discussed previously, even though male MPs had some financial problems, with few exceptions female politicians did not face major financial obstacles. Both men and women mentioned exhausting campaigns, late-night meetings and the serious commitment demanded by political life. However, these were regarded more as inconveniences of the political life that challenged them than as problems.

A few women brought up problems particular to women. Even though these were politicians assuming atypical woman's roles, they had to live up to prevailing conceptions of what a proper woman should do in the society. For instance some women politicians (4 of 12 of the MCMs and 3 of 16 of the MPs) were afraid to be slandered as "loose" women because they were comfortable with their male colleagues or because they wore their skirts"an inch too short." They were under constant pressure to keep a respectable distance from their male counterparts and to dress with excessive modesty. Ece Can said that only after she left politics did she begin wearing sleeveless dresses or going to the beach and wearing swimming suits. During her campaigns she refused to speak while standing on tables in coffee shops, a common practice among men in low-budget Turkish campaigns, because she was afraid she would be jeered at by men who would see her legs. The MC member Handan Yavaş's husband received anonymous telephone calls charging his wife with betraying her husband with a male politician when she was running for office. Even though her husband ignored such calls, Yavaş was demoralized by the slander at a time when she was under heavy electoral pressure. Ironically for the politically aspiring Turkish woman, her atypical career choice could only be successfully pursued by projecting a very typical and traditional image of herself as a faithful and proper wife. While educationally and professionally she was expected to be like her male colleagues, in her manners and behavior she was to project the image of a modest Turkish woman.

Another inconvenience of being a woman in politics was the concern among women about traveling along to distant districts. Although it was not a major problem, at least not one that was insurmountable, some of the women politicians (1 of 12 of the MCMs and 5 of 16 of the MPs) preferred to ask male friends to accompany them when they needed to travel. While traveling with a man was safer, the women had to be careful not to provoke gossip. Male/female relations were carefully censured. Gaye Akdan explained:

I always went with Nedim Bal [a male friend] to give speeches before the elections. We had a Cadillac car. And he would tease me: "Gaye hanım[6] when they see us like this, together in an American car, they won't give us any votes or anything," and I would reassure him, "They will Nedim Bey, they will."[7]

Even though Akdan and Bal relate to each other quite formally as their forms of address—Bey and Hanım—suggest, they were nevertheless concerned, if only to tease each other, that their friendship might be perceived by society as illicit. The woman politician who needed male company for reasons of security at the same time had to maintain the image of a social conformist. Fortunately, at least in the metropolitan areas where the woman politicians ran for office, the need to seek male company when traveling was more a convenience than a necessity. Akdan explained as follows:

> Only when I went far as to Çatalca or to outer districts did I prefer to go along with a male friend or a colleague. Just because it was easier, transportation and everything. Otherwise, in Istanbul I went about by myself.

All the women agreed that they were warmly accepted by the electorate.[8] Even though they were contenders for power competing against men in a society where there were few role models for women in politics, women politicians (15 of 16 of the MPs and 10 of 12 of the MCMs) said that they felt approved of and welcomed by the electorate as eligible representatives. One or two women (1 of 16 of the MPs and 2 of 12 of the MCMs) qualified their responses suggesting that the electorate accepted them gradually, after initial skepticism.

Even though women politicians were welcomed by the populace, they could not really serve as role models. The electorate related to these women as to their sisters, or considered them to be "masculine women." "Bacı" or "abla," terms that mean sister, were applied to the woman politicians. In a country like Turkey where there is still informal segregation between men and women, the sister-brother relationship is a particularly close one. Sisters are usually the only people of the opposite sex that men can relate to as friends.[9] Hence, it was permissible within the prevailing structure of social relations to relate to a woman politician if she were perceived as a sister.

The fact that men and women could relate to women candidates as sisters further suggests that women politicians could not change the electorate's conception of politics as a male realm. Women politicians were addressed as "Mr. Politician." The RPP MP Ece Can who was the bacı and abla of many men and women both older and younger than herself, said that she was also the "Başkan Bey" (Mr. President) when she served as the mayor of the Çatalca Municipality. Although president was a neutral word like chairperson (and unlike the masculine chairman), people assumed that a president had to be a man. Nergis Ney, who was the representative of a remote Eastern Anatolian province for two terms, related this:

They respected me. In fact they called me "hanım bey" [Lady sir].[10] My name became "hanım bey." I'll never forget, in a meeting where my husband was with us, the headman of the village kept on standing up, calling me "hanım bey," talking and talking and sitting down.[11] Once twice, thrice, finally, "Look," I said, "Muhtar bey [sir headman]!" I said, "bey [sir, in reference to the husband] is sitting beside me. I am his hanım [lady, in the context, meaning wife], I am a hanım [lady], I am your representative, but I am a "hanım" [lady]," I said. He stood up again, still very serious. "You," he said, "Since you are our representative to the parliament, you are a bey [sir]," and sat down; they had granted me the title of being a sir. This is, I believe, their way of accepting and supporting women.

As far as her constituents are concerned, Ney is a woman who deserves to be respected like a man because she plays the role of a man. The electorate is willing to respect the woman politician, but denies her the recognition of a new role she is carving out for her gender. The woman politician who is embarking on a new career is nevertheless content to be accepted by the populace, regardless of how they perceive her.

As for male colleagues, women in politics say that they got along with them without any problems. Most of the women politicians (13 of 16 of the MPs and 10 of 12 of the MCMs) agreed that women successful enough to climb the political ladder were respected by their male political colleagues. Winning their male colleagues' respect was a means to political success, as well as an end in itself. Regardless of what men actually thought about women in politics, they seemed to defer to their female colleagues in person. The parliamentarian Beyhan Sunar explained,

Male friends were always very respectful. I was much respected by them. They would listen very carefully when I spoke in parliament. . . . For one thing, they are curious: there are so few women in parliament and you are talking as one of these few women.

Among the MCMs, Ayşe Tar's answer was again very typical,

Male colleagues respected me particularly. Regardless of the party to which they belonged, they would carefully listen and pay attention to what I said as sister Ayse's word.

Even though woman politicians thought that their male colleagues respected them, this formal respect accorded by male politicians to their female colleagues needs to be explored further. Beyond a veneer of respect, men in politics might hinder women's access to political power.

Major Problems in Politics

Male and female politicians who were reticent concerning their own problems would elaborate on why they thought there were so few women in politics. Indeed, they all agreed that women politicians confronted many obstacles. Even though the women interviewed were successful candidates who were elected to offices without much difficulty, they observed other women as having serious problems in politics. Furthermore, they became more conscious of their own problems in response to this question. Table 30 shows the coded answers to the question.[12]

Table 30
Problems Women Have in Politics

	Female MPs	%	Male MPs	%	MCMs	%
Women's Role as a Housewife						
Household duties	3	7.3	1	4.5		
Household interests	2	4.8	1	4.5		
Total	5	12.1	2	9		
Woman's Fault						
Women not interested in politics	1	2.4	1	4.5		
Women don't fight enough and use their opportunities	5	12				
Women don't support each other	2	5	3	13.6	2	7.4
There are few women candidates	2	4.8				
Total	10	24.2	4	18.1	2	7.4
Politics is for men						
Physically tiring for women			4	18		
Women don't have the right attributes			2	9		
Politics is a man's game and women are not tough or vulgar enough to play it	1	2.4	1	4.5		
It is more difficult for women to socialize and have male delegates	5	12	3	13.6	4	14.8

The electorate does not accept women politicians			2	9	
Total	6	14.4	12	54.1	4	14.8
Women don't have the opportunity						
Women don't have the economic power	3	7.3	1	4.5	2	7.4
Women are not educated enough	2	4.8			2	7.4
Men and women are not equal					4	14.8
Total	5	12.1	1	4.5	8	29.6
Men as Obstacles						
Husbands prevent women from active politics	3	7.3	2	9	2	7.4
Male delegates don't take women seriously	5	12	1	4.5	4	14.8
Men pressure women out of politics					2	7.4
The large number of men in politics makes them stronger					2	7.4
Men are already in positions of power which works against women	1	2.4			1	3.7
Men are advantaged against women in political competition	1	2.4				
Rules of the game (meeting times, etc.) favor men	1	2.4				
Men slander women	1	2.4			1	3.7
Men don't want women in politics	3	7.3			1	3.7
Total	15	36.2	3	13.5	13	48.3
Total number of responses	41	100	22	100	27	100

The most striking difference between male and female politicians was that men emphasized that politics was not for women, while women claimed that men kept women from politics. In effect, men and women blamed each other for the small number of women in politics. More than half of the male politicians explained that "politics is too exhausting for women," "women don't have the necessary skills," or "the electorate does not accept the female politician," while only a small proportion of the female MPs and the MCMs could be said to agree. The male MP Galip Far explained,

A woman cooks, she looks after a child. She has to neglect her child. Which husband will concede to this? You came from Beykoz at 2 a.m.

Will the husband claim, "Great, you did a good thing? No man will assume his wife's duties just because she is doing politics. Before anything else, being an MP is an arduous task. A woman cannot endure this. It [being an MP] is carried out man to man. A voter for example, cannot tell a woman that he is unemployed. He'll be reluctant. He won't believe that the woman can shoulder the necessary fight. Also man is more of a demagogue. Demirel [at the time, president of the Justice Party] has come to the pulpit with a stick. Would a woman be able to claim from the pulpit, "This stick is what you have, what I have." Well, I would. A man bullshits. A woman wouldn't be able to do it.

According to Far, politics is a man's game and a woman is not fit for politics. He accepts the traditional sex roles imposed by the society as given and elaborates accordingly. Within this patriarchal vision, a woman cannot choose her private or public responsibilities: "No man will assume his wife's duties." Besides, politics "is carried out man to man." The patriarchal society does not provide her with the resources, whether it be the permission to come home at 2 a.m. or the credibility that being a woman deprives one of in the eyes of the unemployed voter. Perhaps more importantly, she lacks the appropriate language as a source of strength, to swear or to use slang.

Far claims that women's primary household duties keep them away from politics. Many studies in the West also highlight that traditional sex roles and the concomitant responsibilities are a major obstacle for women's success in the public realm.[13] Can women who are recognized as mothers, sisters or wives fullfill the demands of a political career?

Yet, for the woman politicians interviewed these were not important considerations. As discussed earlier, coming from upper or middle class families in a semi-traditional society, these women could afford to hire maids or rely on their mothers and mothers-in-laws to relieve the burdens of their dual roles. They also felt that they were warmly accepted by the electorate. The "kinship culture" in the society allowed these women who could relate to their constituencies as mothers or sisters to assume their new roles.

The overriding problem for the women politicians, however, were the men in politics. When they explained why there were so few women in politics, they most frequently claimed that "men kept women from politics." It was either that male delegates did not take women seriously or that men did not want to have women in politics or else that husbands did not approve of their wives' political participation. Men pressured women out of politics; men's numerical superiority worked against women; they guarded the gates; manipulated the rules of the game in their favor; and they slandered women.

Although the women politicians agreed among themselves more than they agreed with male politicians that men were the major obstacle for women in politics, women MPs mentioned more frequently than MC members that it was also the women's fault that there were so few of them in politics. The parliamentarians charged that women did not use the opportunities they had and did not support one another, or that they did not try hard enough to become candidates. Oya Fer's response was typical in revealing the interrelatedness of the issues in some of the parliamentarians' responses. Ultimately, men blocked women's way, but women had to recognize their culpability, too. She explained,

> We don't know our own strengths as women. First we should recognize our own strengths; of course then, when women begin to recognize their own strengths, men do anything to prevent women from assuming office. They think men have more of a right to assume office. First women should agree on who is a capable candidate and then support her with full force. Men brainwash women [so] that women do not support eligible women but rather support men. Men have the power to influence women: the male politician has the authority and position to promise jobs to mothers in politics for their sons and daughters: "Vote for me, I'll make sure your son has his driver's license."

Although Fer emphasizes how men holding a position of strength can undermine women's efforts at political solidarity, she also recognizes that women need to be better organized. Among the MC members a few agreed that women did not support each other in politics, but it seemed that those who were successful enough to be elected to Parliament expected more from women than did those elected to municipality councils at the local level.

More MC members than parliamentarians thought that men in politics constituted a major problem. The responses of half of the MC members, as opposed to about a third of the MPs, pointed to different ways in which men made it difficult for women to be in politics. Emine Soydam, a MC member who did not have the opportunity to hold political office at the national level, was typically conscious of the ways in which women were disadvantaged in comparison to men. She explained emphatically,

> It is very, very difficult for women to be elected in politics. Men can win over the delegates easily. Tables are set up to wine and dine, sheep are sacrificed. They eat and drink and overnight they can claim all the dele-

gates at the table. A woman cannot do these things. . . . You turn to women and try to secure their support. They say, we do as our husbands tell us to do. Male authority is formidable; that is why the woman always loses, the man wins. First, the husband does not allow the woman to go into politics. Then the women are left to fight each other in the Woman's Branches. Men dictate Woman's Branches anyway. Then when the woman survives all this and aspires to candidacy, they don't take her seriously. "Why vote for a woman when there are all these men?" That is the mentality. If a woman begins to have her presence felt a bit too much among men, they are ready to play with her honor. A woman cannot behave like a man does. If she stays over one night while she is in a remote district, next morning, they'll ask, "Where did this woman stay over last night?" It is not like that when a man stays in a delegate's house. . . . Women would be very successful in politics, if only men let them.

At every stage of a political career men are in better positions to compete with women. The patriarchal structuring of power in society allows men to beat women in politics, Soydam says. Soydam, less willing than the female MPs to acknowledge women's failings, traces the cause of women's problems to male privileges. Other MC members echo Soydam with almost the same words, if not with more resentment. Handan Yavaş explained bitterly,

It is very difficult for women to have themselves accepted in politics. In our world of today, men and women are not equal. Either because we are still Ottomans or else jealousy or something "Why should women assume office when men are around?" "Why should they?" This is the mentality. Supposedly I am one of them, a colleague; but I know I am not. Only when a woman bows to man's authority, do they recognize her. "What if a woman is elected?" They don't even count you in. They see the woman as weak and powerless and in need of protection. And there are many eligible women. . . .

Although women MPs and MC members agree among themselves more than they agree with men as to why there are so few women in politics there are, nevertheless, differences of emphasis among women MPs and MC members regarding the male obstacles to women in politics.

CONVERGENCE OF ATTITUDES

In an attempt to highlight the differences of opinion among the different groups of politicians, similarities should not be overlooked. If we study carefully what the politicians actually say rather than draw attention to what they overtly emphasize, we see that men and women inadvertently reinforce each others' attitudes. Ostensibly formal differences often conceal a striking substantive parallel. For example, when İsmail Or, like many other male MPs, explains how women are not suited to politics, he also reveals how men condescend to women in politics. In other words, Or's condescension helps us understand why women feel men are the major obstacle to women in politics. Or explains,

> Women do not have any effectiveness anyway. They don't put out any work. There are no women who have the power to claim delegates to themselves. Woman's Branches support women and even then they manage to send out barely one representative. Without Woman's Branches, their political representation would drop even more. But actually it is the men who find and bring women into politics anyway. I was the one who put Nevin Bez on the list.[14] I told Ahmet Zil about her.[15]

When asked whether Bez wasn't a particularly powerful candidate in her own right, Or replied,

> Well she did have about a hundred or so delegates, perhaps she was an exception, could have made it to the list on her own. But God forbid, had she not been a woman, they would beat her up in the speaker's chair. Ayla Can too, it was me who suggested that she be the president of the WB. Sude Fal too, had she not joined the district president's clique, she would not have stood a chance. What I mean is that, for women to come anywhere, men have to signal the green light. Otherwise, they can't do it on their own. It is always the men who name the president of Woman's Branches anyway. Politics is a man's domain.

At one level Or argues that politics is not for women. Women do not know how to play the game and in any case, it is the men who bring whatever women politicians there are into politics. At another level, Or gives us an insider's view of what the women perceive as the main male obstacle. Without intending to depict men as a closed power elite that could threaten women, Or describes how men have the power to manipulate women. It is the men who select the Woman's Branches' presidents. Unless men give the green light, he says, women would not be in politics. Even though Or does not mean to suggest that men keep women from politics, he tells us that men do after all have the power to discriminate against women. Despite his own point of view, Or reveals how the male monopoly operates in politics. The problem for women who want to be in politics is their relative weakness with respect to men.

Another example is the male MP, Osman Nuri. He argues that women are not qualified to be in politics. However, the resentment with which he explains himself reveals how women, even when they are qualified to compete with men, might feel, threatened by men.

> Had it been left to me, I would allow no women into the parliament. If I had the licence to pick a hundred people, I would make sure to keep women out of it for the following reason: Women in Turkish society, with the feudal, Ottoman turn of mind, have been conditioned, Even when they cry out, as much as they do, "I exist, I exist," they are bearing witness to their complexes. That is why when they are in positions of authority, they do not and cannot meet their responsibilities. They put on airs, "I am a woman, I can do this." The problem might be that they are simply not brought up to assume the posts they acquire. They won't say, "I am not qualified for this office," or "I have not acquired the necessary skills for this post."

Nuri's contention, "Had it been left to me, I would allow no women into the Parliament," even if exaggerated, could intimidate even the best of the women politicians.

While men unwittingly reveal the nature of the male obstacle women perceive in politics, women allow us to see the extent to which they do not belong to the political realm—that is the male contention regarding women in politics. For example, women politicians admit that they cannot establish a supportive clientele. The female MP Ece Can explains why she believes there are so few women in political office,

> With this election system in force it is very difficult. Egos of men won't let you come through. They'll try to obstruct you at every stage. And you can't claim delegates to yourself. You won't be supported in the primaries. Men are all condescending and, of course, we can't use the opportunities we have either. . . .

Can is most intent to condemn the "egos of men." Yet, between her lines, whatever the extenuating circumstances that make it difficult for a woman of a patriarchal society to establish political networks, Can admits that the women candidates do not have the backing of the delegates. Similarly, when Oya Fer complains,

> Men brainwash women [so] that women do not support eligible women but rather support men. Men have the power to influence women: the male politician has the authority and position to promise jobs to mothers. . . .

Fer concedes to women's lack of political muscle. The patriarchal organization of the society allows men rather than the women to have the authority and position to cultivate political support, but she implicitly concedes that under the circumstances women are not as effective as men in politics.

How Welcome are Women in Politics?

When they explain why there are so few women holding political office, men tell us that whatever the reasons, women do not really fit into the political scene, while women complain that men make them feel that they do not belong. However, when asked whether male politicians prefer male over female candidates, male and female politicians disagree that men are preferred.

Male MPs who eagerly explain how women in politics are unqualified to compete with men unanimously agree that male politicians do not prefer to see a male candidate elected over an equally qualified female candidate. In other words, between a male and a female, who is elected is an open question if the competitors are equally equipped. Male MPs (10 of 10) claim that male politicians do not discriminate against a woman because of her sex.

Women politicians disagree. Most of the female MPs (11 of 16) as well as the MCMs (9 of 12) believe that male politicians discriminate against women and prefer to see the male candidate elected, even when the women are as qualified as the men. There are only a few women (3 of 16 of the MPs and 1 of 12 of the MCMs) who say that men would not discriminate if the competitors are equally qualified.

This disagreement between men and women points to a significant obstacle in women's political participation. If it is actually the case that male politicians, as the women argue, underestimate and discriminate against women in politics, then men are ignorant of their own prejudices. In this case, the problem of male bias becomes an even more insidious problem, more difficult to track down. We know from the previous male responses that such a possibility is real because the men, often inadvertently, revealed their condescension toward women. If on the other hand, contrary to what women argue, men prefer to see male candidates elected only because women are actually less eligible than men, then the problems persist. Women are either reluctant to recognize their faults, or they lack the confidence that, when eligible, they can be accepted in men's political world. Regardless of whether male or female politicians portray the scene more accurately, when male politicians disagree that they discriminate against women and female politicians insist that they do, the lack of mutual understanding is a problem in itself. It is more difficult for men and women to accept each other when they do not share a common perception of the issue.

Overview

In their attempt to rise to the top through political channels, women in Turkish politics, unlike their colleagues in other parts of the world, do not complain of financial difficulties. They do not think that their traditional roles radically undermine their public activities. They believe that the electorate basically accepts them. When they explain why there are so few women holding political office, they play down the importance of these commonly accepted obstacles to election. Yet invincible obstacles remain. According to women politicians, men discriminate against women and keep them out of politics. Even when a woman is as qualified as a male candidate, the women believe the man prefer the male over the female candidate. Ironically, men who, as fathers and husbands, had the authority and privilege to influence their wives and daughters to go into politics were, as male politicians, a source of discouragement for women.

According to men, the case is different. They believe that women are not qualified to hold office and that politics is a male domain. Yet, they claim, if a woman is as qualified as a male candidate, they would not discriminate against her. At this junction, we see a tension between the republican imperative to recognize and include women in a secularized political process, and the patriarchal setting that excludes women from the political realm. While their republican upbringing impels men to condemn discrimination, their patriarchal heritage allows them to think women do not quite belong to the political world. The male assurance of women's political inefficacy contributes to their manipulative behaviour, thereby rendering women ineffective in politics. This induced inefficacy is then regarded by men as proof that women are in themselves incapable of effective political action. While men fail to recognize their role in determining the position of women in politics, women tend to isolate the cause of their weakness in the biases of men. In either case, the lack of a mutual understanding between men and women is hardly beneficial to the latter's political careers.

8
Conclusion

Patriarchy: A Catalyst or an Obstacle to Change?

In this book, I attempted to study women politicians in Turkey using a theoretical framework developed by feminist writers. My aim was twofold: to understand how women move from the private to the political world in Turkey, and to see the extent to which patriarchal explanation could shed light on the issue. As such I was applying a framework developed in the West to a context in which it had not been applied before.

By patriarchy, I meant a structure of power that endorses male supremacy. I assumed that as imbalanced power structures where men dominate, patriarchal relationships impede women's political activities. My interviews revealed the paradoxical nature of women politicians' patriarchal ties in Turkey. Men shaped women's political participation at different stages of their social and political life; however, this shaping meant that men facilitated as well as obstruced women's political involvement. The unequal power relation between men and women that was a handicap at the macro level was instrumental in drawing women into politics at the micro level.

Turkish society is undeniably patriarchal. The legal system, though recognizing the basic equality of men and women, nevertheless subtly discriminates against women. Educationally, two thirds of all men, in contrast to half of all women, know how to read and write. Roughly about a third of the primary and secondary school graduates are women. At the higher education level, the percentages of women drop to a quarter of the graduates. The ratio of educated women with respect to men has not improved significantly since the foundation of the republic. In the labor force, there have always been fewer women than men. Of those women in the labor force, more than 90 percent are in agriculture. Industrial and service sectors of the economy are sharply segregated such that women work only in certain industries or services. Male authority prevails in the family as well. Men and women claim that fathers or husbands have more authority than mothers or wives. Even when women have economic independence, male authority retains its dominant status in the family. All channels of cultural expression endorse and perpetuate male authority over women. Novels, plays, school books, and more importantly, radio and television project values and stereotypes that subtly or overtly reinforce practices that sustain the patriarchal society. Identified as their fathers' daughters and their husbands' wives, women define themselves within this system of patriarchy. In the realm of politics, men again monopolize political authority. Surveys and interviews show that women vote as their male relatives do and adopt the political views of their husbands and fathers. In parliament, the percentage of women dropped from 4.5 percent in 1935—the first election year women became eligible to vote and be elected to political office—to 0.9 percent in the 1970s.

In this male dominated society, women representatives benefited from men's power until they competed for office. Historically men promoted women's rights even though there was no women's movement pressuring for these rights. The founding fathers of the republic initiated the necessary legal changes and named women to electoral lists. With this patriarchal backing, women entered the political arena.

The few women who held office over the years were the privileged who had the same, if not better, economic and educational opportunities that men did. Only those who could acquire the individual resources in education and economic means could aspire to a successful political career. Yet, existence of opportunities for higher education and economic well being were necessary, but not sufficient conditions for women's access to political office.

In the private domain, male support was crucial for women's political involvement. Supportive husbands and fathers who shared their power and authority with their family members were the norm in the families of women who attained positions of political power. Typically, in a Turkish family fathers are recognized as the sole authority. However, the politicians interviewed perceived their fathers as unassuming authoritative figures who consulted family members on decision making. These undominating patriarchal figures were the critical figures in drawing women into politics. Only a few women became politically involved on their own. Fathers and husbands kindled the political interest of these women. Many who did not intend to become politically involved were recruited into politics by male politicians.

The authority these supportive male figures could claim accounted for their influence over women's initiation into politics. It was not merely the roles these men assumed as fathers, husbands and politicians or the socialization process behind such roles, but rather the authority they could assume within these roles that was critical. Without this supportive male authority, women might not have been in politics. Unlike their male colleagues, women politicians did not spontaneously respond to political events. Even when exposed to the same political events and media as men—which was the case for a number of women interviewed, especially those who had a university education—women did not see politics as congenial to their interests. Patriarchal norms had shaped women's expectations to be fulfilled outside the political domain. The ideology of politics as the business of men was not easily dismantled in a society where men had traditionally dominated the political realm.

Once in politics, women confronted many problems because of their gender. Most of them could not establish the politically efficacious links that would be assets in parliamentary elections. It was easier for a man to relate to the mostly male delegates to establish the patronage links that could be assets in elections. Being a woman was a disadvantage when staying overnight in election campaigns or in wining and dining with the delegates. Even women who had long years of successful party work at upper levels of the party echelons were at times appointed to the primary lists after unsuccessful attempts to secure the necessary delegate backing on their own.

When asked why there were so few women in politics, both men and women politicians elaborated on women's problems in politics. Men emphasised that women were politically ineffective, whereas women complained that men were responsible for their lack of success. Interestingly, when questioned on the existence of male discrimination against women in politics, men vehemently denied that there was any, whereas women insisted that men discriminated against them. There was little speculation on men's part that they might be unaware of their biases and on women's part that they might have been excluded because they were not qualified competitors. Nevertheless this lack of symmetrical perception of women's problems in politics was not conductive to women's increased political participation. Women in politics had to survive within a web of problems spun by the preponderant male authority in socioeconomic and political life.

The patriarchal structure's power is better appreciated in the context of women's initiation into the political realm. When observing the unequal distribution of power at different layers of society, it is easy to ignore the significance of this power in allowing women to collaborate in maintaining the structure. Opportunities women acquire within the patriarchal society unwittingly compel women to further legitimize and perpetuate the system. Women enter politics not merely on men's terms, but also because men motivate them. As such they are given the occasion to partake in the patriarchal pie. They have stakes in perpetuating the system that allows them to exercise political power. After all, women have made a patriarchal deal.

Yet, ironically women do not totally succumb. The mechanism of dominance manifested in Turkish patriarchalism provides only a medium of finite possibilities for women whereby men promote as well as impede women's progress. And even women who have become part of the system are keenly aware of the unequal male power working against them. Women's dissatisfaction with the system allows us to speculate on prospects for change. Before we do that, we can briefly reconsider our explanation of women politicians' patriarchal bind and consider the implications of women's political representation.

Alternative Explanations?

In the context of the interview data, the unequal power relationship between men and women could help to explain different aspects of women's political involvement. The male/female power dynamics was a central dimension of women's political involvement. Yet, unlike what the patriarchal explanation led us to expect, the disproportionate power of men could be instrumental in initiating the individually endowed women into politics. From the viewpoint of women politicians, men were both a vehicle as well as a hindrance, depending on the context in which they related to women.

Could alternative explanations besides patriarchal theory elucidate the dynamics of women's political involvement as well, so that our understanding of women's political careers would be enhanced? It is true that men might not have played such an important role in women's political careers had they not been socialized to play their male roles as socialization theory would suggest. A similar suggestion could be made regarding the socialization of women. Nevertheless, it is not merely any role that men or women have that is of significance in women's political careers, but rather the power and authority that is associated with the roles men and women assume in accordance with their gender. It is because they are men, for example, that fathers and husbands or political rivals have the powers to promote or obstruct women. In the final analysis, it is these powers men command, not merely the roles they assume that determine men's capacity for effective action. The authority that is attributed to their gender explains the influence men playing different roles have over women.

Moreover, the sex-differentiated learning process in society is perpetuated because men have the power they do, not merely because of the roles they assume. Conceivably men could assume the same roles and do not have the privileges they do to perpetuate a socialization process which, in turn, preserves these privileges. However, because of their gender, men who assume these roles have the power to enforce the traditional socialization process.

Focusing on the different dimensions of power dynamics between men and women offers an alternative to the Marxist approach. It is necessary to identify the power discrepancy between genders to understand how men can obstruct as well as promote women in politics. Yet the male authority that shapes women's political participation is not simply a product of class inequality. The inequality between men and women is determined not merely by their relationship to production but rather to reproduction. And this inequality based on gender is critical in explaining how women can or cannot move from the private to the public realm. We thus claim that patriarchal theory offers insights into the issue of women's political participation that other theories might not have.

Impact or Contribution of Women Parliamentarians

In an attempt to study how women move from the private realm to positions of political leadership in Turkey, we have not explored the consequences of this move. Because the number of women in the Turkish Parliament has always been very small (highest number was 4.5 percent of the Parliament), it is not realistic to expect women as a group to have a significant impact on the policy making process and the development of legislation. Four or five women of different political parties are not likely to unite to take effective action in the Parliament. Yet, when we study the parliamentary records to find out in what manner women have contributed to parliamentary debate, not necessarily to see how they have shaped the outcome of that debate, we see a change of pattern over time. Since 1935 when suffrage was granted, the content as well as the style of speeches women parliamentarians have delivered in the public parliamentary debates has changed.

During the first decade after suffrage was granted (1934–45), women who served in the Parliament perceived themselves as representatives of women. In fact, they were chosen as parliamentarians by the ruling elite precisely because they were women. They spoke on behalf of women, to introduce women's perspectives on issues that were discussed in the parliamentary debate. They frequently prefaced their statements with phrases like, "As a Turkish woman," or "As women."[1]

Interested as they were to express the women's viewpoint, women parliamentarians of this era were not involved in promoting the so called, "woman's cause." Questions of equal opportunity or sex role changes were not at issue. Without a feminist movement to highlight these questions, women parliamentarians much like the other women they represented were oblivious to such concerns. Yet, they dutifully voiced opinions on issues concerning traditional women's fields. They asked questions and expressed their views on debates about child care, child punishment, education and family policies.[2]

With the advent of the multiparty era (1945–60), the ruling elite who promoted women's rights lost power. Women elected during this period under increasingly competitive conditions were, nevertheless, symbols of legitimation for the competing political parties. Yet, these women did not see themselves primarily as representatives of women anymore.[3] Speeches were not delivered to state women's viewpoints. There was no attempt to draw attention, to being women representatives. On the contrary, the women MPs were merely partisans participating in the sharp rivalry between the DP and the RPP. The political stands they assumed faithfully reflected their primary party loyalties.[4] What still continued, however, was their interest in issues concerning traditional women's interests, namely, child rearing, health and educational policies.[5]

Between 1960–1980, women elected to the Parliament began to take an active interest in diverse issues, besides those associated with traditional women's roles. While their numbers were few (lowest since 1935 in ratio to men), the women MPs of this era had mostly worked in the party cadres, had been nominated by the party delegates to be selected to office and had survived competition with men. In the assembly, they could represent their parties not merely as individual party members, but also as group speakers. They delivered speeches on a broad range of issues from foreign policy to economic recovery, from U.S.-Turkish relations to the budget talks.[6] Issues on traditional women's fields were still within the range of topics, women MPs covered in Parliament, but not exclusively.[7]

Women parliamentarians of the 1960–80 era could represent diverse interests in Parliament because of the experiences they gained in socio-economic and political life. Compared to the women MPs of the earlier periods, they had longer political careers. In addition, they were more at home dealing with socio-economic problems in a society where the republican reforms on women's rights were bearing fruit. These few privileged women could, then, have similar experiences to men and express interest in the same issues men did. In other words, it was not a feminist upheaval or a concern with equal representation that prompted women's increasing involvement in a broad spectrum of societal problems. Under the special circumstances women came to power, and with the patriarchal bind they were in, the best they could do was to become like men. Their impact as *women* politicians was bound to be limited, as they became more like their competent male counterparts.

Prospects

The problem of women's small numbers in politics remains. The impact of women representatives in politics is bound to be limited within the confines of the system in which they move from the private to the political realm.

A public policy oriented response to the problem would be to recommend that the state be mobilized to facilitate women's political involvement.[8] To this end, the government could undertake or subsidize programs that promote equality. In the short run, affirmative action could be a temporary means to assure equal participation and representation of women in socio-economic life. In the long run, measures could be taken to educate men and women for democratic citizenship. Training programs could be set up to encourage women's entry into the labor market.

These policy recommendations assume that increased education and increased participation in the labor force help to increase the number of women who become politically involved. Clearly, there is no direct relationship between either education and labor force participation or labor force participation and political participation. Education per se may not improve labor force participation and increased labor force participation may not politicize women.[9] The prevailing structure of society mediates the potentially liberating effects of these variables. In our sample we could see that most of the educated professional women were not spontaneously drawn into politics.

Yet, both education and labor force participation are nevertheless avenues that might be instrumental in politicizing women. An education for democratic citizenship that encourages women's political activism might prompt women to work outside the home. A stable employment might insure the economic independence necessary, if not sufficient for political activism. At work, women exposed to new issues and experiences might develop a sense of efficacy that can then be translated into the political realm. Increased labor force participation might also increase women's stakes in politics and, hence, increase their numbers in politics. It is, after all, only in those countries where feminist movements precipitated radical changes in the positions of women through increased education and employment outside the home that women's representation in politics has risen.[10] Nevertheless the tentative nature of these prospects needs to be underlined.

Hypotheses about the relationship between education, labor force participation, and politics need to be tested in their appropriate contexts. A complementary follow-up study that would shed light on the issues and questions raised in this work would be one that focuses on the workplace. How do a sample of professional women, women doctors or lawyers for example, move from the private to the public realm? What are the problems they confront in their professional lives? Are these problems a result of their gender? How do we compare the problems women politicians as opposed to women professionals confront? Did professional involvement spark political interests at any stage in their careers? If not, an attempt could be made to understand the specific causes of this apathy and alienation from politics. The results might be further compared with a similar study on a group of female factory workers. To understand why there are so few women in politics, and how they move from the private to the political realm, it is essential to examine the experiences of women who are not in politics and those who are clearly apolitical.

Yet, public policy recommendations or research on women who are not in politics are not enough to address the issue of women's initiation into the political realm. At this point, further speculation is needed as to why it is important to explain the lack of women in politics. A popular awareness of the significance of the issue precedes any serious move that can be made. The low numbers of women in Turkish politics indicates that there is no political will to bring about any change and no clear vision as to why the issue is important such that the political will necessary to take effective action can be mustered.

As discussed in chapter 1, there is no set consensus among feminists as to why women should move into political office. Increased women's representation can be considered an end in itself. Democratic norms dictate that women participate equally with men in political decision making concerning their common lives. We might argue that women's political representation should be promoted without further consideration of its implications so that women can learn to govern themselves along with men.

Yet, does this move involve a denial of women's identity? As many female politicians testify to and many feminists criticize, the process of assuming positions of political leadership within the present institutions can iron out differences based on gender. Women might enter political office only when they have become like men, not merely in qualifications necessary to assume office but also in their political style and priorities. Hence, women succumb to male power and exercise power like men do. The feminists should seek to uphold women's "separate as well as equal" status to men.

Accordingly, women in politics can and should represent women's interests in a diverse manner. On political issues—war and peace included—they can introduce the women's perspective. Experiences women acquire in their traditional roles can help them contribute to the development of educational and family policies. they can promote specific women's issues such as abortion, paternity leaves and equal rights. In short, they can help to change the political discourse.

However, when women enter the political arena to represent women's interests, there is always the danger that the sexual division of labor in society be duplicated in the political realm to the detriment of women. Women thus might not get the opportunity to move beyond issues related to the reproductive realm to exercise their will on questions concerning the productive realm. Rather than change the political discourse, they might be trapped in it.

It is among these alternatives that women must articulate their goals regarding their role in politics. If the normative issue as to who and what the women representatives should represent is better defined, it might precipitate change to bring more women into the political realm. The Turkish case—where women lack such direction—shows that otherwise women are easily constrained within the bounds of patriarchy. Patriarchal organization of society is deeply entrenched and strong precisely because women cooperate in preserving it. A new vision that assesses the rewards and punishments patriarchy offers women under the prevailing conditions and one that provides new alternatives for the future can promote change. After all, even those who individually benefit from an exercise of patriarchal power are dissatified with its prevalence. With a widespread and better articulated vision, women can be ready to question the nature of their political commitments and seek to reestablish those structures that shape their access to the political realm.

Appendixes

Appendix A
Year of Universal Suffrage

Turkish women obtained suffrage in 1935. The following is a list of countries in which suffrage was granted prior to and after that date.

BEFORE 1935		AFTER 1935	
Finland	1906	France	1944
Britain	1918	Hungary	1945
Denmark	1915	Italy	1945
Iceland	1915	Japan	1945
USSR	1917	Belgium	1948
Austria	1919	Canada	1948
Poland	1919	Israel	1948
USA	1920	Syria	1949
Spain	1931	Mexico	1953
		Egypt	1956
		Pakistan	1956
		Lebanon	1957
		Libya	1963

Source of data: Elise Boulding et al., *Handbook of International Data on Women* (New York: Halsted Press, John Wiley and Sons, 1976), p. 250.

Appendix B
Women Representatives to the Grand National Assembly

Last name, First name	Term	Education	Occupation
1. Gönenç, Mebrure	5	shs (ACG)	Mersin Municipality Council member
2. Çırpan, Satı	5	literate	agriculture/headman
3. Baştuğ, Türkân	5	u	president, Üsküdar Girl's Technical School
4. Gökçül, Sabiha	5	u	president, İzmir Girl's Teacher Training School
5. İnsel, Şekibe	5	jhs	agriculture

Last name, First name	Term	Education	Occupation
6. Öniz, Huriye	5	u	teacher
7. Memik, Fatma	5	u	doctor
8. Elgün, Nakiye	5	shs	Istanbul City Council member/teacher
9. Öymen, Fakihe	5	u	high school president
10. Arıman Benal	5	u	city council member/RPP Advisory Council member/teacher
11. Güpgüp, Ferruh	5	jhs	RPP Advisory Council
12. Morova, Bediz	5	jhs	municipality council member
13. Pektaş, Mihri	5	shs (ACG)	language teacher
14. Ulaş, Meliha	5	u	high school teacher
15. Nayman, Esma	5	shs	language teacher/municipality council member
16. Görkey, Sahiba	5	u	high school teacher
17. Hızal, Seniha	5	u	Girl's Technical School teacher
18. Özgener, Hatice	5	jhs	president, junior high school
1. Gönenç, Mebrure	6	shs	politics
2. Baştuğ, Türkan	6	u	teacher
3. Gökçül, Sabiha	6	u	teacher
4. Memik, Fatma	6	u	doctor
5. Elgün, Nakiye	6	shs	politics/teacher
6. Öymen, Fakihe	6	u	teacher
7. Arıman, Benal	6	u	teacher/politics
8. Pektaş, Mihri	6	shs	teacher
9. Baykan, Belkıs	6	u	senior high school teacher
10. Yunus, Şehime	6	u	İzmir Girl's High School teacher/Halkevi president
11. Dicle, Hacer	6	shs	teacher/municipality council member
12. İşcan, Şemsa	6	u	city council member
13. Gürleyük, Mergube	6	jhs	municipality council member
14. Develi, Muammer	6	u	dentist
15. Abanozoğlu, Salise	6	shs	Trabzon Girl's School teacher
1. Gönenç, Mebrure	7	shs	politics
2. Gökçül, Sabiha	7	u	teacher
3. Memik, Fatma	7	u	doctor
4. Elgün, Nakiye	7	shs	politics/teacher
5. Öymen, Fakihe	7	u	teacher
6. Arıman, Benal	7	u	teacher/politics
7. Pektaş, Mihri	7	shs (ACG)	teacher
8. Baykan, Belkıs	7	u	teacher
9. Yunus, Şehime	7	u	teacher/politics
10. İşçan, Şemsa	7	u	city council member
11. Develi, Muammer	7	u	dentist
12. Abanozoğlu, Salise	7	shs	teacher

Last name, First name	Term	Education	Occupation
13. Aksoley, Mebrure	7	u (law)	RPP Çankaya Ocak president
14. Ilgaz, Hasene	7	shs	teacher/RPP District Advisory Council member
15. Taşkıran, Tezer	7	u	teacher
16. Kâğıtçılar, Saadet	7	u	doctor/İzmir City Council member
1. Öymen, Fakihe	8	u	teacher
2. Arıman, Benal	8	u	teacher/politics
3. Aksoley, Mebrure	8	u	politics
4. Ilgaz, Hasene	8	shs	teacher/politics
5. Taşkıran, Tezer	8	u	teacher
6. Budunç, Zehra	8	shs	RPP Bursa Advisory Council member
7. Çeyrekbaşı, Latife	8	shs	teacher/İzmir Municipality Council member
8. Dıblan, Makbule	8	u	doctor
9. Mollaoğlu, Zekiye	8	u	Istanbul Girl's Lycee math teacher
1. Taşkıran, Tezer	9	u	teacher
2. Tlabar, Nazlı	9	shs (ACG)	DP Beyoğlu ilçe president
3. Adıvar, Halide Edip	9	shs (ACG)	teacher
1. Tlabar, Nazlı	10	shs (ACG)	politics
2. Coşkun, Aliye Temuçin	10	shs	teacher
3. Pınar, Nuriye	10	u	teacher
4. Sayar, Edibe	10	u	lawyer
1. Tlabar, Nazlı	11	shs (ACG)	politics
2. Pınar, Nuriye	11	u	teacher
3. Elli, Übeyde	11	shs	RPP Central Women's Branch president
4. Levent, Piraye	11	u	pharmacologist/DP provincial advisory council member
5. Ulman, Hilâl	11	u	teacher
6. Günel, Ayşe	11	shs	teacher/Istanbul Municipality Council member
7. Tekinel, Necla	11	u	lawyer/Istanbul Municipality Council member
8. Arıburun, Perihan	11	u	lawyer
1. Gedik, Melahat	1	u	lawyer
2. Evren, Saadet	1	u	lawyer
3. Ağaoğlu, Neriman	1	shs	housewife

Last name, First name	Term	Education	Occupation
1. Gedik, Melahat	2	u	lawyer
2. Ağaoğlu, Neriman	2	shs	housewife
3. Gürsoy, Nilüfer	2	u	teacher
4. Seçkin, Türkan	2	shs	teacher/Edirne RPP WB president
5. Düşünsel, Sevinç	2	u	lawyer/NTP Central Advisory Committee member
6. Neftçi, Nermin	2	u	lawyer, Eminönü district president
7. Boran, Behice	2	u	teacher/TLP president
8. Koçak, Zarife	2	shs	teacher/RPP Central Advisory Council member

Last name, First name	Term	Education	Occupation
1. Neftçi, Nermin	3	u	lawyer/politics
2. Tural, Suna	3	u	teacher
3. Gülşen, Zekiye	3	u	teacher/administrator
4. Tokgöz, Zarife İkbal	3	u	lawyer/JP WB president
5. Akarca, Mualla	3	u	agricultural engineer/politics

Last name, First name	Term	Education	Occupation
1. Öztürk, Feriha	4	shs	MC member
2. Gülsen, Zekiye	4	shs	teacher/administrator
3. Köksal, Aliye	4	shs	housewife
4. Gürsoy, Nilüfer	4	u	teacher
5. Mankut, Gülhiz	4	u	lawyer/politics
6. Tok, Şükriye	4	shs	politics

Last name, First name	Term	Education	Occupation
1. Ege, Çağlayan	5	shs	politics
2. Korum, Sevil	5	u	economist
3. Gürsoy, Nilüfer	5	u	teacher
4. Uğural, Ayten	5	u	lawyer

Women Representatives to the Senate

Last name, First name	Term	Education	Occupation
1. Şahingiray, Özer	1	u	head librarian
2. Akarca, Mualla	1	u	agricultural engineer

Last name, First name	Term	Education	Occupation
1. Akarca, Mualla	2	u	agricultural engineer
2. Aksoley, Mebrure	2	u	politics
3. Tüzün, Zerrin	2	u	Girl's Teacher Training School president

Last name, First name	Term	Education	Occupation
1. Tüzün, Zerrin	3	u	administration
2. İşmen, Fatma Hikmet	3	u	agricultural engineer
3. Üçok, Bahriye	3	u	teacher

Last name, First name	Term	Education	Occupation
1. İşmen, Fatma Hikmet	4	u	agricultural engineer
2. Belül, Solmaz	4	u	lawyer
3. Ayda, Adile	4	u	ambassador
1. Abadan-Unat, Nermin	5	u	teacher
2. Baykal, Aysel	5	u	lawyer
3. Ayda, Adile	5	u	ambassador

KEY TO SYMBOLS:

u   university
shs   senior high school
jhs   junior high school
ACG American College for Girls

Appendix C
Sample

The sixteen female MPs whom I interviewed shared with their female parliamentary colleagues of the multiparty era similar educational, professional, and regional backgrounds. The sixteen women interviewed were highly educated professionals, most of whom were not elected from the province in which they were born. The majority, eleven out of sixteen, were representatives of the three metropolitan cities: Istanbul, seven; Ankara, three; and Izmir, one. Their educational and occupational status is summarized in tables 1 and 2.

About 60 percent of the women MPs elected during the multiparty era had university degrees, and 40 percent were professionals.

Table 1
Female MPs Interviewed: Education

	Terms Elected		
Degrees Held	1946–60	1960–80	Total
University	1	7	8
Senior High	3	5	8
Total	4	12	16

Table 2
Female MPs Interviewed: Occupation

	Terms Elected		
Occupation	1946–60	1960–80	Total
Law	3	4	4
Teaching		2	5
Professional other than law		2	2
Housewife		1	1
Held political office prior to election	1	3	4
Total	4	12	16

Among those interviewed, 50 percent were university educated and 37 percent professionals. Almost half the women (7 out of 16, that is, 44 percent) were married, a slightly lower percentage than the average among the female MPs (62 percent).

RPP representatives were overrepresented in the sample. Nine of the sixteen women were affiliated with the RPP, three with the DP, and two with the JP. During the multiparty era, 21 RPP, 12 DP and 11 JP members were elected. One woman was from the Turkish Labor Party and one from the New Turkey Party.

Eleven out of the sixteen held office for only one term and four for two terms. The average age of the women at the time they entered parliament was 44.

Eight out of ten male MPs interviewed had university degrees, much like the 84 percent of the Istanbul MPs and the 75 percent of the post 1960 male MPs. Seven out of the ten were lawyers. While this figure is higher than the corresponding figure for the male universe (36 percent among Istanbul MPs, about 40 percent among post 1960 MPs nationwide), it does reflect the trend towards greater representation by lawyers. Tables 3 and 4 show the educational and occupational status of the ten MPs. Only three of these ten were born in Istanbul, whereas 60 to 70 percent of the MPs elected after 1960 represented the provinces in which they were born. Like most male MPs, all the men in my sample were married. There were seven RPP and three JP representatives, which made the male sample biased in favor of the RPP much like the female sample. Six of the ten male MPs served for one term and the other four two or more terms. Their average age at the time of entry into the parliament was 46, two years older than the female average of 44.

The twelve women MC members interviewed were closely representative of the 51 women MC members elected (after 1960) in Ankara and Istanbul. These women were less educated and had fewer professionals among them than the women elected to the parliament. Tables 5 and 6 show their educational and occupational status.

Table 3
Male MPs Interviewed: Education

Degree	Number
University	8
Senior High	1
Elementary	1
Total	10

Table 4
Male MPs Interviewed: Occupation

Occupation	Number
Law	7
Professional other than law	1
Business/Trade	1
Union related	1
Total	10

Table 5
Female MC Members Interviewed: Education

Degree	No. in Istanbul	No. in Ankara	Total
University	2	2	4
Senior High	2	2	4
Junior High	2	2	4
Total	6	6	12

Table 6
Female MC Members Interviewed: Occupation

Occupation	No. in Istanbul	No. in Ankara	Total
Housewife	3	4	7
Law	1	1	2
Teaching	1		1
Other	1	1	2
Total	6	6	12

Appendix D
Interview Schedule

Name:
Marital Status:
Children:
Place of Birth:
Date of Birth:
Education:
Occupation:
1. How did you become an MP? Could you tell me about it?
   a. When did you become politically involved?
   b. Can you recall or specify the event that was most significant in your initiation into politics?
   c. Were there any people who particularly motivated, encouraged/discouraged you in becoming politically involved? In assuming office? Who were they?
   d. Did you have close friends or relatives in politics before you became politically involved?
2. Why did you want to run for office?
3. In your election campaigns, what themes did you use to address the electorate?
   a. (if women) Did you try to address women in particular?
4. What kinds of problems if any did you have when you tried to be elected?
   a. Did you feel that your gender made things easier or more difficult for you? How?
   b. Did you have financial problems in the election?
5. Why do you think you were able to be elected to office?

IN OFFICE

1. (if women) Did you feel that your gender made things easier or more difficult for you, in office?
   a. Did you have any problems relating to, or working with, male colleagues?
2. What issues did you work on when in office?
3. (if women) Did you have a female constituency who preferred to ask favors from you rather than from a male representative because you were a woman?
4. Did you regularly socialize with male or female colleagues?
5. Do you think your male colleagues prefer to nominate or see elected equally qualified male as opposed to female politicians?
6. Did you enjoy being in office? Why?
7. Would you have liked to be in office for another term? Why?
   a. Did you try to get reelected?
8. Whom do you consider yourself to be representing when in office?
9. What did you think of your male colleagues?
10. What did you think of your female colleagues?

SOCIAL/POLITICAL ATTITUDES

1. There are few women in Turkish politics. Why do you think that there are so few women politicians?
2. Should there be more women politicans? Why?
3. What do you think of the Woman's Branches of the major parties?
4. Why do you think that there are not more women with jobs?
5. Would you rank higher in prestige a representative of the National Assembly, a professor, a doctor?

BACKGROUND

1. Do you have brothers and/or sisters?
   a. (if women) In what ways did you feel you were treated differently from your brothers, if you had any, or from male children in general?
2. Could you tell me about your mother?
   a. Did she work outside the home?
   b. Was she religious (i.e., perform the five daily prayers regularly)?
   c. Did/does she follow politics closely?
3. Could you tell me about your father?
   a. What was his occupation?

b. Was he religious (i.e., perform the five daily prayers regularly)?
c. Did/does he follow politics closely?
4. How would you describe the political atmosphere at home?
5. Who had the final word on disciplinary issues within the family?
   a. Was there strict discipline at home, which, for example, in-
      volved punishment?
   b. What kind of punishment, if any, was meted out?
6. Did your father or mother affect your career choice?
7. Who decided on choices that involved a lot of money such as
   housing, buying a car or having a vacation? The father, the
   mother, your parents together, your parents after consulting the
   children?
8. Would you say you came from a lower/middle/upper middle/
   upper class family?

SOCIAL LIFE

1. If married, at what age did you get married?
   a. What is your spouse's occupation?
2. Did marriage change your life plans? How?
   a. Did you earn your own living after your marriage?
3. How did election to political office affect your private life?
4. If you had children, who looked after them?
5. Who has the authority on disciplinary issues regarding the children?
6. Does your spouse help with the housework? How?
7. Who decides on the issues that involve a lot of money such as
   housing, buying a car, or having a vacation?
8. Would you consider yourself lower/middle/upper middle/upper
   class family?
   a. Do you own or rent the apartment you live in?
9. Were you or are you a member of any social organizations?
   Which ones?

VALUES

1. Do you enjoy discussing politics in your private life?
2. Do you like to avoid or engage in political discussions with people who disagree with you?
3. Would you rather be respected for your independent opinions or
   for your ability to get along well with people?
4. What kind of person would you like your daughter to be?
5. What would you say your personal or political goal in life is at
   present?

Appendix E
Women Candidates According to Parties in Post-1960 Elections to the National Assembly

Table 1

1961 OCCUPATION	JP	RPP	RPNP	NTP
Housewife	3	1	4	1
Lawyer	2	1	1	1
Teacher	1	1	3	
Academic Career			1	2
Administration			1	2
Writer			2	
Total	6	3	12	6

Table 2

1965 OCCUPATION	JP	RPP	NAP	NP	TLP	NTP
Housewife	1	2	4	3	3	4
Lawyer	1	5	1	2	1	2
Teacher		2	2		2	4
Academic Career	2				1	2
Administration			1	1	1	
Writer			1	1		3
Other Professional					1	2
Total	4	9	9	7	9	17

The appendix has been compiled from the following issues of *The Official Gazette* (*Resmi Gazete*): 30 September 1961, 13 September 1965, 15 September 1969, 17 September 1973, 7 May 1977.

Table 3

1969 OCCUPATION	JP	RPP	NP	TLP	NTP	RP	NAP	UP
Housewife		4	1	1	12	6	7	5
Lawyer	2	2	3					
Teacher			2	2	1			
Academic Career			3	2	1	4		
Administration	2	1	3		3			
Writer				2	1			
Other Professional	1			1	1			1
Total	5	7	12	8	19	10	7	6

Table 4

1973 OCCUPATION	JP	RPP	NP	RRP	NAP	TLP	DP
Housewife		3	4	4	9	3	5
Lawyer	2		1	1			1
Teacher			1	2	1		
Academic Career		1		1			1
Administration	2	2		3	1		1
Writer					1		
Other Professional							
Total	4	6	6	11	12	3	8

Table 5

1977 OCCUPATION	JP	RPP	RRP	NAP	DP	TLP
Housewife			1	11	1	
Lawyer	1	4	1			
Teacher	1		7			
Academic Career	2	1	2			1
Administration	3	1	15		6	
Writer					2	
Other Professional			2	1	1	
Worker						2
Total	7	6	28	12	10	3

KEY TO PARTY NAMES:

JP	Adalet Partisi (Justice Party)
RPP	Cumhuriyet Halk Partisi (Republican People's Party)
RPNP/NP	Cumhuriyet Köylü Millet Partisi (Republican Peasants' Nation Party) Millet Partisi (Nation Party)
NTP	Yeni Türkiye Partisi (New Turkey Party)
TLP	Türkiye İşçi Partisi (Turkish Labor Party)
RP/RRP	Güven Partisi/Cumhuriyetçi Güven Partisi (Reliance Party/Republican Reliance Party)
NAP	Milliyetçi Hareket Partisi (National Action Party)
DP	Demokratik Parti (Democratic Party)
NSP	Milli Selamet Partisi (National Salvation Party)
UP	Birlik Partisi (Union Party)

Appendix F
Self-Evaluations by Interviewees of Masculine and Feminine Characteristics

Developed by Sandra L. Bem, this sex-role inventory allows individuals to evaluate themselves on a scale from 1 (never true) to 7 (always true) about adjectives that commonly possess masculine, feminine, or neutral connotations.* The following is the mean of self-evaluations by the interviewees on this inventory.

FEMININE	MP female	MP male	MCM female
Yielding	1.8	1.6	2.3
Cheerful	5.0	4.9	5.9
Shy	1.8	2.4	1.3
Affectionate	6.4	5.7	6.7
Flatterable	2.3	2.2	1.6
Loyal	6.8	6.5	6.8
Feminine	3.6	1.3	3.2
Sympathetic	6.0	6.2	6.5
Sensitive to the needs of others	6.5	6.9	6.9
Understanding	6.0	6.8	6.5
Compassionate	6.1	6.8	6.9
Eager to soothe hurt feelings	6.5	6.7	7.0
Soft-spoken	4.5	6.4	6.5
Warm	5.3	6.4	6.5
Tender	4.9	4.2	4.3
Gullible	2.9	2.0	2.9
Childlike	1.7	2.4	3.9
Does not use harsh language	6.1	5.0	5.4
Loves children	6.1	6.2	6.9
Gentle	6.1	5.8	5.1

*Bem, Sandra L. "The measurement of Psychological Androgyny." *Journal of Consulting and Clinical Psychology* 42, no. 2 (February 1974): 15–162.

MASCULINE	MP female	MP male	MCM female
Self-reliant	6.1	6.7	6.6
Defends own beliefs	6.5	6.8	6.9
Independent	6.1	6.6	6.9
Athletic	3.7	4.0	2.8
Assertive	6.1	6.5	6.9
Strong personality	6.5	6.8	6.7

Forceful	6.2	6.1	5.3
Analytical	6.3	4.6	4.6
Has leadership abilities	5.5	5.3	4.8
Willing to take risks	6.0	6.4	5.5
Makes decisions easily	4.6	5.0	5.0
Self-sufficient	6.2	6.7	6.9
Dominant	6.0	6.3	5.4
Masculine	2.3	6.2	2.4
Willing to take a stand	3.3	3.6	2.5
Aggressive	2.0	1.5	1.7
Acts as a leader	5.8	5.8	5.4
Individualistic	2.6	1.5	1.3
Competitive	2.6	2.7	3.4
Ambitious	3.6	3.8	2.3

NEUTRAL	MP female	MP male	MCM female
Helpful	6.3	6.6	7.0
Moody	2.2	2.2	1.2
Conscientious	6.9	7.0	6.8
Theatrical	1.8	2.2	1.2
Happy	5.3	5.6	5.5
Unpredictable	2.0	2.0	1.0
Reliable	6.8	6.8	6.9
Jealous	1.5	4.4	1.2
Truthful	6.7	6.8	6.9
Secretive	6.3	6.3	6.6
Sincere	6.8	6.8	6.9
Conceited	2.0	2.2	1.0
Likable	5.9	6.25	6.7
Solemn	6.26	6.4	6.9
Friendly	6.6	6.6	6.9
Inefficient	2.3	3.5	2.5
Adaptable	6.5	6.5	6.7
Unsystematic	2.8	4.4	3.2
Tactful	5.8	6.3	5.6
Conventional	5.4	5.1	4.2

Notes

Preface

1. Works by the following authors throw different lights on the questions. Jeane Kirkpatrick, *Political Woman* (New York: Basic Books, 1974); Rita Mae Kelly and Mary Boutilier, *The Making of Political Women* (Chicago: Nelson Hall Inc., 1978); Marcia Lee, "Toward Understanding Why Few Women Hold Public Office," in *A Portrait of Marginality: The Political Behavior of the American Woman*, ed. Marianne Githens and Jewel L. Prestage (New York: McKay, 1977), pp. 118–38; Lynne Iglitzin, "The Making of the Apolitical Woman: Femininity and Sex-Stereotyping in Girls," in *Women in Politics*, ed. Jane Jaquette (New York, Wiley, 1974), pp. 25–36; Susan J. Pharr, *Political Women in Japan* (Berkeley: University of California Press, 1981); Cynthia Fuchs Epstein and Rose Laub Coser, eds., *Access to Power: Cross-National Studies of Women and Elites* (London: George Allen Unwin, 1981); Ruth Mandel, *In The Running* (New York: Ticknor and Fields, 1981); Elina Haavio-Mannila et al., eds., *Unfinished Democracy: Women in Nordic Politics* (Oxford: Pergamon Press, 1985); Drude Dahlerup, ed., *The New Women's Movement* (London: Sage Publications, 1986).

2. The debate is elaborated in Chapter 1, Introduction: Patriarchy and Women in Politics in this work.

3. Even though Turkish women, especially those in politics, have not been studied to the extent that Western women have been, there is a growing interest among Turkish social scientists in women's research. A landmark in providing analytical perspective on different aspects of women in Turkey is a collection of essays edited by Nermin Abadan-Unat, *Women in Turkish Society* (Leiden: E.J. Brill, 1981). Çiğdem Kâğıtçıbaşı, ed., *Sex Roles, Family and Community in Turkey* (Indiana: Indiana University Turkish Studies, 1982) is a later collection with insightful articles that have a firm indigenous grounding. Ferhunde Özbay, ed., "The Study of Women in Turkey: An Anthology" (unpublished manuscript, 1985) is the most recent collection and has a concise review article by the editor. Specifically on women and political participation, there is only one serious work: Şirin Tekeli, *Kadınlar ve Siyasal-Toplumsal Hayat* (Women and sociopolitical life) (Istanbul: Yaylacık Matbaası, 1982). Tekeli's is a comprehensive study of women in sociopolitical life. An attempt is made to employ Marxist analysis to explain disparate facets of women's political activity.

4. Further discussion of the sample is in chapter 4.

5. Richard Bernstein, *The Restructuring of Social and Political Theory* (Philadelphia: University of Pennsylvania Press, 1978), pp. 229–30.

Chapter 1. Introduction: Patriarchy and Women in Politics

1. Hester Eisenstein and Alice Jardine, eds. *The Future of Difference* (New Brunswick, N.J.: Rutgers University Press, 1985); Mary Fainsod Katzenstein and David D. Laitin, "Politics, Feminism and the Ethics of Caring," in Eva Feder Kittay and Diana Meyers, eds., *Women and Moral Theory* (Totowa, N.J.: Rowman and Littlefield, 1987).

2. Ellen Carol DuBois, *Feminism and Suffrage* (Ithaca: Cornell University Press, 1978), pp. 16–17. On the general question of sex equality, see Jane English, ed., *Sex Equality* (Englewood Cliffs, N.J.: Prentice-Hall, Inc., 1977).

3. Eisenstein and Jardine, *Future of Difference*; Katzenstein and Laitin, "Politics."

4. Nancy Cott elaborates the concept of women's sphere in *The Bonds of Womanhood: "Woman's Sphere" in New England, 1780–1835* (New Haven: Yale University Press, 1977).

5. Barbara Bellow Watson, "On Power and the Literary Text," *Signs* 1, no. 1 (Autumn 1975): 111.

6. On political socialization see: Fred Greenstein, "Political Socialization," *International Encyclopedia of the Social Sciences*, ed. David Sills (New York: Macmillan Company and Free Press, 1968–79), 14: 552; H. Hyman, *Political Socialization* (Glencoe, Ill.: Free Press, 1959). For a critical evaluation see R. W. Connell "Why the 'Political Socialization' Paradigm Failed and What Should Replace It," in *International Political Science Review* 8. no. 3 (1987): 215–23. On the way political socialization approach is used in women's studies see Lynne Iglitzin, "The Making of the Apolitical Woman: Feminity and Sex-Stereotyping in Girls," in Jaquette, *Women in Politics*, p. 30. Also, Kelly and Boutilier, *Making of Political Woman*; Anthony Orum et al., "Sex, Socialization and Politics," in Githens and Prestage, *Portrait of Marginality*, p. 30.

7. Examples of "role structures" explanations can be found in Seymour Martin Lipset, *Political Man* (New York: Doubleday and Co. Inc., 1963), p. 206, and Jeane Kirkpatrick, *Political Woman*.

8. On Marxist explanations in women's studies see, Lorrenne M.G. Clark, "The Consequences of Seizing the Reins in the Household: A Marxist Feminist Critique of Marx and Engels" in Judith H. Stiehm, ed., *Women's Views of the Political World of Men* (New York: Transnational Publishers Inc., 1984) pp. 179–203. For the Marxist debate on women's status see, Margaret Benston, "The Political Economy of Women's Liberation," *Monthly Review* 21, no. 4 (1969): 13–27. The Marxist argument introduced by Benston has been developed by Wally Seccombe, "The Housewife and her Labor under Capitalism," *New Left Review*, no. 83 (January–February 1973), and "Domestic Labor, a Reply to Critics," *New Left Review*, no. 94 (November–December 1974); Jean Gardiner, "Women's Domestic Labor" *New Left Review*, no. 89 (January–February 1975); Margaret Coulson, Branka Magas, and Hilary Wainwright, "The Housewife and her Labor under Capitalism," *New Left Review*, no. 89 (January–February 1975).

9. Simone de Beauvoir, *The Second Sex* (New York: Knopf, 1953); Viole Klein, *The Feminine Character* (Chicago: University of Illinois Press, 1971); Kate Millet, *Sexual Politics* (New York: Doubleday and Co., 1969); Shulamith Firestone, *The Dialectic of Sex* (New York: William Morrow and Co. Inc., 1970); and Zillah Eisenstein, *The Radical Future of Liberal Feminism* (New York: Longmans Inc., 1981).

10. Millett, *Sexual Politics*, p. 25.

11. See Lorenne M.G. Clark and Lynda Lange, *The Sexism of Social and Political Theory* (Toronto: Toronto University Press, 1979), pp. vii–xii.

12. Ibid.

13. Max Weber, *Economy and Society*, ed., Max Rheinstein (Cambridge: Harvard University Press, 1954), p. 323. Also see Reinhard Bendix, *Max Weber* (Berkeley: University of California Press, 1977) pp. 294,332.

14. Although patriarchal dominance in society is recognized as legitimate male authority rather than naked power dominance, it is legitimate not because it is just, but because it is lawful and conforms to societal norms for reasons discussed in the text. The process of legitimation transforms power, which, according to its dictionary definition, means the ability to do or to act, into authority, that is, the rightful ability to do so.

15. Michel Foucault, *History of Sexuality* 1 (New York: Pantheon Books, 1978), p. 92.

16. Ibid, p. 93.

17. Kelly and Boutilier, *Making of Political Woman*; Mandel, *In the Running*, and Lee, "Why Few Women Hold Public Office" in Githens and Jewel, *A Portrait of Marginality*; Lynda Watts Powell, "Male and Female Difference in Elite Political Participation: An Examination of the Effects of Socio-economic and Familial Variables, " *The Western Political Quarterly* (March 1981).

18. Kelly and Boutilier, *Making of Political Women*. Powell, *Elite Political Participation*.

19. For maternal influence over the politics of the daughter see Pharr, *Political Women in Japan*. Also see Nancy Chodorow, *The Reproduction of Mothering: Psychoanalysis of Gender* (Berkeley: University of California Press, 1978) for the argument that the close relationship between mothers and daughters perpetuates the traditional division of labor between the sexes.

Chapter 2: Patriarchy in Turkish Society

1. Tezer Taşkıran, *Cumhuriyetin 50. Yılında Türk Kadın Hakları* (Turkish women's rights in the fiftieth year of the republic) (Ankara: Başbakanlık Basımevi, 1973), p. 125.

2. My focus is on urban women because their traditions are more pertinent for my study of women in politics. Urban women were different from rural women who formed the pillars of the agricultural economy. Besides working in the fields, rural women prepared cotton and tobacco products for industrial processing. See Lütfü Erişçi, *Türkiye'de İşçi Sınıfının Tarihi* (History of the working class in Turkey) (Istanbul: Kutulmuş Basımevi, 1951), p. 11. Turkish carpets were almost all woven by women; see Charles Issawi, *The Economic History of Turkey 1800–1914* (Chicago: Chicago University Press, 1980), p. 311.

3. Even though I shall not discuss the nature and causes of these changes, I should note that improvements in the status of women were part of the general process of modernization under the impact of economic pressures, Western influence, and wars; however, Europeans were not interested in pressuring the Ottomans for change in the status of women per se. See Bernard Lewis, "Tanzimat and Social Equality" in Jean Louis Bacqué-Grammont and Paul Dumont, eds., *Économie et Sociétés dans L'Empire Ottoman* (Paris: Editions du Centre National de la Recherche Scientifique, 1983), pp. 47–54.

4. This interpretation does not account for the historical and cultural rationale

of these Islamic precepts. Such precepts can be interpreted in the context of a liberal theocracy, vide Ali Shariati. See Adele K. Ferdows "Women and the Islamic Revolution," *International Journal of Middle Eastern Studies* 15 (1983), pp. 283–98. I write from a secular and republican perspective and hence overlook alternative (Islamic) interpretations.

5. See under Nikah ("Marriage"), *The Encylopedia of Islam* (EI), ed. M.Th. Houtsma (Leiden: Brill, 1927), 3, pt. 2, pp. 912–14.

6. My transliterations conform to Turkish usage, not Arabic.

7. Entry for *talak*, in *EI*, 4, pt. 2, pp. 636–40.

8. Entry for *zina*, in *EI.*, 4, pt. 2, p. 1227; Reuben Levy, *The Social Structure of Islam* (Cambridge: Cambridge University Press, 1969), pp. 119–20, for kanun contrary to sharia on adultery, p. 268. See also Taşkıran, *Cumhuriyetin 50.*, p. 46.

9. See under Abd ("Slave"), *The Encyclopedia of Islam*, new edition, ed. H.A.R. Gibb (Leiden: Brill, 1960), 1, pp. 24–40; on slavery in the modern period and abolition, pp. 34–37.

10. It must be noted, however, that the decrees were initially quite ineffective. See ibid.

11. Ibid., p. 37.

12. Reuben Levy, *Social Structure of Islam*, pp. 96–7.

13. Ömer Lütfü Barkan, *Türk Toprak Hukuku Tarihinde Tanzimat* (Tanzimat in the History of Turkish Land Law) (Istanbul: Maarif Matbaası, 1940), p. 26.

14. Jan Dengler, "Turkish Women in the Ottoman Empire," in *Women in the Muslim World*, ed. Lois Beck and Nikki Keddie (Cambridge: Harvard University Press, 1978), p. 230.

15. On decrees concerning women's attire, see T.Z. Tunaya, *Islamcılık Cereyanı* (The Pan-Islamic Movement) (Istanbul: Baha Matbaası, 1962), p. 101; also Taşkıran, *Cumhuriyetin 50.*, p. 29; Bernard Caporal, *Kemalizmde ve Kemalism Sonrasında Türk Kadını* (Kemalist and Post-Kemalist Turkish Woman) (Ankara: TISA Matbaası, 1982), pp. 143–45.

16. "Harem," in *Encyclopedia of Islam*, new ed., 3, p. 209.

17. N. Penzer, *The Harem* (Great Britain: J.B. Lippincott Co., 1936), p. 175.

18. Lady Mary Wortley Montagu, *The Complete Letters of Lady Mary Wortley Montagu*, ed. Robert Hasband (Oxford: Clarendon Press, 1965), 1, p. 363.

19. Lucy Garnett, *Women of Turkey and Their Folk-Lore* (London: David Nutt, 1893), pp. 472–73; also Hester Donaldson Jenkins, *Behind Turkish Lattices* (London: Collins' Clear Type Press, n.d.) pp. 9–17.

20. Garnett, *Women of Turkey*, p. 263.

21. Ülkü Bates, "Women as Patrons of Architecture in Turkey," in Beck and Keddie, *Women in the Muslim World*, p. 256.

22. *Tasviriefkar*, 1867, no. 457, in A. Hamdi Tanpınar, *Namık Kemal Antolojisi* (Istanbul: Tan Matbaası, 1942), p. 38. Unless specifically noted to the contrary all translations from Turkish are my own.

23. Lucy Garnett, *Turkish Life in Town and Country* (London: George Newnes Ltd., 1904), p. 60.

24. Faik Reşid Unat, *Türkiye'de Eğitim Sisteminin Gelişmesine Tarihi Bir Bakış* (A historical look at the development of the educational system in Turkey) (Ankara: Milli Eğitim Basımevi, 1964), pp. 6–9.

25. Boys had access to such senior high schools (sultaniyes) as Galatasaray and Darüşşafaka, a university (dar-ül-fünun), a medical school, and a civil servant school (Mülkiye). Bernard Lewis, *The Emergence of Modern Turkey* (London: Oxford University Press, 1961), p. 182, 229.

144   THE PATRIARCHAL PARADOX

26. Taşkıran, *Cumhuriyetin 50.*, p. 27.
27. Unat, *Türkiye'de Eğitim Sisteminin*, pp. 35–36.
28. Ibid., p. 80.
29. Halide Edip Adıvar, *Memoirs of Halide Edip Adıvar* (New York: The Century Co.), p. 6
30. Abd, *Encyclopedia of Islam*, pp. 24–40.
31. From the 1913 and 1915 *Industrial Statistics* (Istanbul, 1917), quoted in Lütfü Erişçi, *Türkiye'de İşçi Sınıfının*, pp. 11–12; see also Charles Issawi, *Economic History of Turkey*, p. 313.
32. Ibid., p. 7. It is possible that many of these momen were non-Muslims.
33. Taşkıran, *Cumhuriyetin 50.*, p. 40. Lewis, *Emergence of Modern Turkey*, p. 238.
34. Ibid.
35. Ibid., pp. 40–43.
36. Ibid., pp. 38–39.
37. Namık Kemal, "Terbiyei Nisvân Hakkında Bir Layihadan" (From a document on the education of women), *Tasviriefkar*, 1867, no. 457, in *Tanpınar, Namık Kemal Antolojisi*, p. 39.
38. Niyazi Berkes, *The Development of Secularism in Turkey* (Montreal: McGill University Press, 1964), p. 390.
39. *Türkiye'de Dergiler-Ansiklopediler (1849–1984)* (Journals and encyclopedias in Turkey, 1849–1984) (Istanbul: Gelişim Yayınları, 1984).
40. Erişçi, *Türkiye'de İşçi Sınıfının*, p. 11.
41. Taşkıran, *Cumhuriyetin 50.*, pp. 68–73; these speakers were educated middle-class women.
42. Afet Inan, *Tarih Boyunca Türk Kadınının Hak ve Görevleri* (The history of the rights and responsibilities of Turkish women) (Istanbul: Milli Eğitim Basımevi, 1975), pp. 108–25.
43. Ibid., pp. 127–28.
44. See Caka Cahit, *Tarih Boyunca Harp ve Kadın* (War and women in history) n.p., n.d., pp. 57–77.
45. Taşkıran, *Cumhuriyetin 50.*, p. 81.
46. Şerif Mardin, "Ideology and Religion in the Turkish Revolution" *International Journal of Middle East Studies* 2 (1971): 239.
47. See Berkes, *Development of Secularism*, pp. 461–78.
48. Afet İnan, *Atatürk Hakkında Hatıralar ve Belgeler* (Memoirs and documents on Atatürk) (Ankara: Türk Tarih Kurumu Basımevi, 1959), p. 259.
49. Taşkıran, *Cumhuriyetin 50.*, p. 67.
50. Dankwart A. Rustow, "Atatürk as Founder of a State" *Daedalus* (Summer 1968), pp. 816–18.
51. John Patrick Douglas Balfour Kinross, *Atatürk: The Rebirth of a Nation* (London: Unwin Brothers Ltd., 1964) pp. 418–24.
52. Tekeli, *Siyasal-Toplumsal Hayat*, p. 216.
53. Ibid., pp. 214–16.
54. Ibid., p. 215.
55. Lewis, *Emergence of Modern Turkey*, pp. 267–68, 292.
56. See Taşkıran, *Cumhuriyetin 50.*, pp. 52–61 for excerpts concerning women from the writings of these intellectuals; also Berkes, *Development of Secularism*, pp. 389–90, on women's status and emancipation.
57. See Berkes, *Development of Secularism*, pp. 388–90.
58. Ibid., pp. 388–90.

59. *Atatürk'ün Söylev ve Demeçleri* (Speeches and declarations of Atatürk), 2, 1906–1938) (Ankara: Türk Tarih Kurumu Basımevi, 1952), p. 85.
60. Quoted from Osman Ergin, *Türkiye Maarif Tarihi* 5 (History of Education in Turkey) (Istanbul, 1943), pp. 1501–4, in Berkes, *Development of Secularism*, p. 470.
61. See Berkes, *Development of Secularism*, p. 390; for Ziya Gökalp's precepts on women, p. 390.
62. *Atatürk'ün Söylev ve Demeçleri*, 2, p. 152.
63. Ibid., p. 86.
64. Ibid., p. 86.
65. Ibid., p. 150, from the Konya speech given on 21 March 1923.
66. İnan, *Atatürk Hakkında Hatıralar ve Belgeler*, p. 251.
67. The Commission for the Amendment of the Civil Code has proposed a new code that alleviates some of the weaknesses discussed. Şirin Tekeli reviews the proposal critically in "Kadınların İsteği 'Özgürleşme' mi 'Eşitlik' mi? Medeni Kanun Tartışmalarının Düşündürdükleri" (Do women want "liberation" or "equality?" Considerations on the civil code debate), *İktisat Dergisi* (Journal of Economics) (May 1985), pp. 46–50.
68. Deniz Kandiyoti, ed., *Major Issues on the Status of Women in Turkey: Approaches and Policies* (Ankara: Çağ Matbaası, 1980), p. 59.
69. Ülker Gürkan, "Türk Kadınının Hukuki Statüsü ve Sorunları" (Legal status and problems of Turkish women) *Ankara Üniversitesi Hukuk Fakültesi Dergisi* 35, no. 1–4 (Ankara: Ankara Üniversitesi Basımevi, 1981).
70. Devlet İstatistik Enstitüsü (D.İ.E.) (State Institute of Statistics), *Genel Nüfus Sayımı* (Population census of Turkey), 26 October 1975; 1 percent sample results (Ankara: D.İ.E. Matbaası 1976), pp. 8–11, chart 4.
71. Calculated from above statistics.
72. Elise Boulding, et al., *Handbook of International Data on Women* (New York: Halsted Press, John Wiley and Sons, 1976), p. 134.
73. Ibid., pp. 145–7, 154. Turkey is ranked 86.5 among 134 countries classified according to percentage of women in primary and secondary education. It is ranked 89.5 among 129 nations compared according to the percentage of women in higher education.
74. Calculations based on data from Kandiyoti, ed., *Status of Women*, p. 36.
75. See Ferhunde Özbay, "The Impact of Education on Women in Rural and Urban Turkey," in Abadan–Unat, ed., *Women in Turkish Society*, for a more detailed discussion of the relationship between rural/urban residence and the benefits derived from educational opportunities.
76. DİE, *Genel Nüfus Sayımı* (1975), p. 18 table 8.
77. Ibid., p. 18.
78. Most of the women are unpaid family workers. Nikki Keddie makes the argument that methods of Turkish census takers must provide the most accurate figures for female rural employment in the Middle East. See Nikki K. Keddie, "Problems in the Study of Middle Eastern Women," *International Journal of Middle East Studies* 10, no. 2 (1979): p. 237.
79. Kandiyoti, *Status of Women*, p. 20, table I.
80. DİE, Genel Nüfus Sayımı, p. 46, chart 40.
81. Ibid., p. 107, chart 96.
82. DİE 1 percent sample results, *Genel Nüfus Sayımı*, pp. 22–23, chart 9.
83. Ayşe Öncü, "Turkish Women in the Professions: Why So Many?" in Abadan-Unat, *Women in Turkish Society*, pp. 182–84. Although official statistics

on practicing engineers do not record sex distinction, we can estimate that women engineers are not as numerous as lawyers and doctors on the basis of the number of women graduates in engineering, which totaled 8 to 9 percent in 1970s; DİE, Genel Nüfus Sayımı.

84. U.S. Bureau of the Census, *Statistical Abstract of the United States, 1979* (100th edition) no. 687, (Washington D.C.: U.S. Government Printing Office 1979), p. 416.

85. *Statistisches Jahrbuch 1981 für die Bundesrepublik Deutschland* (1981 Statistical Yearbook for the Federal Republic of Germany) (Berlin: Bundesdruckerei, 1981), p. 323, chart 15.3.

86. Boulding et al., *Handbook of International Data*, pp. 159–60.

87. U.S. Bureau of the Census, *Statistical Abstract*, p. 416.

88. Bundesrepublik Deutschland, *Statistisches Jahrbuch*, p. 323.

89. See for example, the Polish figures cited by Magdalena Sokolowska, "Women in Decision Making Elites: The Case of Poland," in Epstein and Coser, *Access to Power*, p. 104.

90. Öncü, *Turkish Women in the Professions*, pp. 188–90.

91. Ibid., pp. 188–90.

92. DİE, *Genel Nüfus Sayımı*, pp. 22–23.

93. U.S. Bureau of the Census, *Statistical Abstract*, p. 416.

94. Bundesrepublik Deutschland, *Statistisches Jahrbuch*, p. 323.

95. DİE, *Genel Nüfus Sayımı*, pp. 22–23.

96. U.S. Bureau of the Census, *Statistical Abstract*, p. 416.

97. See Serim Timur, *Türkiye'de Aile Yapısı* (Family structure in Turkey) (Ankara: Hacettepe Üniversitesi Yayını, 1972).

98. Çiğdem Kâğıtçıbaşı, *Çocuğun Değeri* (Value of children) (Istanbul: Boğaziçi Üniversitesi, Gözlem Matbaacılık Koll. Şti., 1981), p. 85.

99. Timur, *Türkiye'de Aile Yapısı*; Mübeccel Kıray, *Ereğli: Ağır Sanayiden Önce Bir Sahil Kasabası* (Ereğli: a coastal town before heavy industry) (Ankara: T.C. Başbakanlık Devlet Planlama Teşkilatı, 1964).

100. Constantina Safilios-Rothschild, "The Study of Family Power Structure: A Review 1960–1969," in *Journal of Marriage and the Family* 32 (November 1970): pp. 539–52.

101. Ibid; Robert Blood and Donald Wolfe advanced the resource theory in *Husbands and Wives* (New York: Free Press, 1960).

102. Emelie A. Olson, "Duofocal Family Structure and an Alternative Model of Husband and Wife Relationship" in Kâğıtçıbaşı, ed., *Sex Roles, Family and Community*, pp. 33–72.

103. Paul J. Magnarella, "Conjugal Relationships in Modernizing Turkish Town," *International Journal of Sociology of the Family* II, no. 2 (September 1972): 179–91. Also see Paul Magnarella, "Aspects of Kinship Change in a Modernizing Turkish Town," *Human Organization* 31, no. 4 (Winter 1972): 361–71.

104. Greer L. Fox, "Another Look at the Comparative Resources Model: Assessing the Balance of Power in Turkish Marriages," *Journal of Marriage and the Family* 35 (November 1973): 718–30.

105. Kâğıtçıbaşı, *Sex Roles, Family and Community*, p. 87.

106. Timur, *Türkiye'de Aile Yapısı*, p. 103.

107. Ibid., p. 103.

108. Ibid., p. 107.

109. Kâğıtçıbaşı, *Sex Roles, Family and Community*, p. 85.

110. Ibid., p. 85.

111. Frederick Frey, "Socialization to National Identification Among Turkish Peasants," *Journal of Politics* 30 (1968): 964.

112. Beşir Atalay, *Köy Gençliği Üzerinde Sosyolojik Bir Araştırma* (A sociological survey on village youth), no. 525, (Ankara: Üniversitesi Yayını, n.d.), p. 138.

113. Ibid., p. 138.

114. Ibid., p. 142.

115. Oya Tokgöz, *Siyasal Haberleşme ve Kadın* (Political communication and women) (Ankara: Sevinç Matbaası, 1979).

116. Ibid., p. 186.

117. Ibid., p. 217.

118. Ahmet Taner Kışlalı, "Siyasal Tutumlarda Kuşak ve Cinsiyet Etkenleri" (Sex and age as determinants of political attitudes) *Ankara Üniversitesi, Siyasal Bilgiler Fakültesi Dergisi* 31, nos. 1–4 (March–April 1976), p. 117.

119. Ibid., p. 117.

120. E. Kemal Eyüboğlu, *Şiirde ve Halk Dilinde Atasözü ve Deyimler* (Proverbs and Maxims in Poetry and Folk Language) (Istanbul: Doğan Kardeş Matbaacılık Sanayii, 1973), p. 34. Also, Şirin Tekeli, "Halk Deyişlerinde Kadın" (Women in Folk Sayings) *Somut* Haziran 1983 No. 19/20; reprinted in *Cumhuriyet Dönemi Türkiye Ansiklopedisi* İletişim Yayınları 5. p. 1198.

121. I used Eyüboğlu for the proverbs quoted in this section.

122. *Türkiye Cumhuriyeti Milli Eğitim Bakanlığı İlkokul Programı* (Republic of Turkey, ministry of national education elementary school program) (Istanbul: Milli Eğitim Basımevi, 1968), p. 216.

123. Ibid., p. 262.

124. Ibid., pp. 374, 388.

125. *Türkiye Cumhuriyeti Milli Eğitim Bakanlığı Ortaokul Programı*, (Republic of Turkey, ministry of national education junior high school program) (Istanbul: Milli Eğitim Basımevi, 1970), p. 45, and *Türkiye Cumhuriyeti Milli Eğitim Bakanlığı Lise Müfredat Programı* (Republic of Turkey, ministry of national education senior high school program) (Ankara, 1973), pp. 125–33.

126. For a discussion of women in Turkish literature, see Füsun (Altıok) Akatlı, "The Image of Women in Turkish Literature," in Abadan-Unat, *Women in Turkish Society*, pp. 223–32.

127. *Hayat*, 16 October 1969, 43, p. 10.

128. Ibid., 11 December 1969, 51, p. 15.

129. See daily newspapers such as *Milliyet, Hürriyet* between 5 and 30 October 1981, especially the *Milliyet* series "Karı mı Koca mı" (Husband or wife), 12–18 October 1981, p. 7.

130. Mete Akyol, "Karı mı Koca mı," *Milliyet*, 12 October 1981, p. 7.

Chapter 3: Politics and Office Holding by Women

1. Wilma Rule, "Why Women Don't Run: The Critical Contextual Factors in Women's Legislative Recruitment," *The Western Political Quarterly* 34, no. 1, (1981), pp. 73–76.

2. Torild Skard and Elina Haavio-Mannila "Women in Parliament" in Haavio-Mannila et al., eds., *Unfinished Democracy: Women in Nordic Politics* (Oxford: Pergamon Press, 1985).

3. See Walter Weiker, *Political Tutelage and Democracy in Turkey* (Leiden: Brill, 1973). On the evolution of the parliamentary system in Turkey see Ahmet

Yücekök, *Türkiye'de Parlamento'nun Evrimi* (Evolution of the Parliament in Turkey) (Ankara: A.Ü.S.B.F. ve Basın Yayın Yüksek Okulu Basımevi, 1983) especially pp. 149–236. Also, Feroz Ahmad, *The Turkish Experiment in Democracy, 1950–1975* (London: C. Hurst and Co., 1977).

4. Nermin Abadan-Unat, *1965 Seçimleri Tahlili* (An Analysis of the 1965 Election) (Ankara: Sevinç Matbaası, 1966), p. 70.

5. Ibid., p. 70.

6. T. Erdem, ed., *Seçim Kanunları* (Election Laws) (Istanbul: Şevket Ünal Matbaası, 1973).

7. B. Lewis, *Emergence of Modern Turkey*, pp. 384–400.

8. Sabri Sayarı, "Aspects of Party Organization in Turkey," *The Middle East Journal* 30, no. 2 (Spring 1976): 189.

9. Secondary literature on WBs is almost nonexistent. For the interaction between the RPP Central Executive Committee and WB, see Suna Kili, *CHP'de Gelişmeler* (Developments in the RPP) (Istanbul: Çağlayan Basımevi, 1976), pp. 153–54, 288. Also see Suna Kili, "CHP'de Tüzük Tasarısı ve Gençliğe Yönelik Çelişkiler" (The RPP program draft and contradictions concerning youth), *Milliyet*, 12 November 1976, p. 2.

10. *Adalet Partisi Kadın Kolu Programı* (Program of the Justice Party woman's branch) (Ankara, 1963).

11. *Cumhuriyet Halk Partisi Kadın Kolu Programı* (Program of the Republican People's Party woman's branch) (Ankara, 1969).

12. Robert D. Putnam, *The Comparative Study of Political Elites* (Englewood Cliffs, N.J.: Prentice Hall, 1976), pp. 22–28; also Suzanne Keller, *Beyond the Ruling Class: Strategic Elites in Modern Society* (New York: Random House, 1963), p. 121.

13. Frederick Frey, *The Turkish Political Elite* (Cambridge: MIT Press, 1965), p. 12.

14. Frederick Frey, "Patterns of Elite Politics in Turkey," in *Political Elites in the Middle East*, ed. George Lenczowski (Washington, D.C.: American Enterprise Institute for Public Policy Research, 1975), p. 57.

15. In the 1973 parliament, the percentage of teachers in the "officials" category increased to 8.7 percent; however, professionals still constituted 44.3 percent, and "officials" 27.5 percent of the Parliament. See Frank Tachau, "Social Backgrounds of Turkish Parliamentarians," in *Commoners, Climbers, and Notables*, ed. C.A.O. Van Nieuwenhuijze (Leiden: Brill, 1977), p. 296.

16. Ibid., p. 60.

17. On patron-client networks in Turkey, see Sabri Sayarı, "Political Patronage in Turkey," in *Patrons and Clients in Mediterranean Societies*, ed. Ernest Gellner and John Waterbury (London: Duckworth, 1977).

18. The table is constructed from the parliamentary albums of the relevant years.

19. United Nations General Assembly 25th Session, 15 December 1970, table 2. With the exception of Nordic countries, most nations have a low number of women representatives. Women constitute about 5 percent of the national legislators in most parliamentary democracies. The figure is no higher in the central committees of the Communist Party in countries such as China and Russia. In the United States, the percentage of women in the Congress increased from about 2 percent in the 1930s to 4 percent in the late 1970s. Possible exceptions are the Scandinavian countries in which effective government policy and effective women's movements reinforce each other. In Norway the figures were 7 percent in 1957 and 24 percent

in 1977. In Finland the total changed from 14 percent in 1962 to 26 percent in 1979. See Putnam, *Political Elites*, pp. 33–34. Also see Skard and Haavio-Mannila, "Women in Parliament" in Haavio-Mannila, *Unfinished Democracy*; Skard, "Progress for Women: Increased Female Representation in Political Elites in Norway," in Epstein and Coser, *Access to Power*, p. 78; Haavio-Mannila, "Women in the Economic, Political and Cultural Elites in Finland," in Epstein and Coser, *Access to Power*, p. 57. Also see, for comparative data on women in national legislatures, *Women in the World Today*, U.S. Department of Labor, International Report I, 1963.

20. The two municipalities are in metropolitan cities not representative of rural areas; I was unable to gain access to a comprehensive record of provincial municipalities. Public libraries did not have municipality council albums. At the Istanbul and Ankara municipalities, I saw only post-1960 records, which were more accessible than those for previous years.

21. The tables are compiled from the parliamentary albums; Appendix I provides a more detailed list.

22. Senators, required by law to have a university education, are excluded.

23. See Şirin Tekeli, "Women in Turkish Politics," in Abadan-Unat, *Women in Turkish Society*, p. 305. Tekeli claims that compared to men "women are the much better educated group." However, she uses the figures of Frey (1965) for 1920 to 1957 to calculate the percentage of educated men, which do not take into consideration the higher rates of the later years. Frey's followup article (1975), which I have used, is inclusive of later trends.

24. Table compiled from *Istanbul Belediyesi Meclis Albümü* (Istanbul municipality album), 1963, 1968, 1973, 1977.

25. Compiled from the parliamentary albums.

26. Compiled from the Istanbul municipality albums.

27. Compiled from the parliamentary albums.

28. Rule, *Why Women Don't Run*, pp. 73–76.

Chapter 4: Who Are the Women Politicians?

1. Gaetano Mosca, *The Ruling Class*, ed. Arthur Livingston, (New York: McGraw Hill, 1939), p. 53.

2. Of these forty women, thirty-two were representatives to the National Assembly and eight to the Senate which was founded in 1961. Although the DP was established in 1946, most observers consider 1950 as the beginning of the multiparty era.

3. Of the forty, five were dead, three were sick, four were out of the country, three declined to be interviewed, and seven could not be located during the time period the study was carried out.

4. During the same period five women held five seats.

5. For the interview questions see Appendix D.

6. All the names have been changed to assure anonymity.

7. At the time of his election $1 (U.S.) = 20 £T.

8. In Turkey, law is not as highly paid a profession as it is in the U.S.

9. Kenneth P. Langton, *Political Socialization* (London: Oxford University Press, 1969); Kelly and Boutilier, *Political Women*, chapter 5.

10. Safilios-Rothschild, *The Study of Family Power Structure*.

11. These women explained further that their fathers were usually absent—one

a railroad worker who was always away from home, another a dilettante who had a mistress, another dead.

12. To summarize and compare the degree of patriarchal authority in the families of these three groups of politicians, I attempted to standardize the answers given to the two questions on parental authority within the family. I constructed an elementary index whereby I assigned numerical values to the politicians,' responses, the highest value, 4, corresponding to those answers which indicated the most authoritative position of the fathers. The lowest value of 0 was assigned to those answers that showed that mothers had the sole authority or decision making power. Accordingly, the averages that were calculated were as follows; female MPs, 5.0; male MPs, 7.4; female MC members, 3.4.

13. Şerif Mardin, "Religion in Modern Turkey" *International Social Science Journal* 29, no. 2 (1977), Binnaz Toprak, *Islam and Political Development in Turkey* (Leiden: Brill, 1981).

14. İlkay Sunar and Binnaz Toprak, "Islam in Politics" *Government and Opposition* 18, no. 4 (Autumn 1983).

15. See Tansı Şenyapılı, "Metropol Bölgelerin Yeni Bir Ögesi Gecekondu Kadını" (A New Element of Metropolitan Regions: Woman of Squatter Settlements), in Abadan-Unat, ed., *Women in Turkish Society*, pp. 295–97.

16. See Timur, *Türkiye'de Aile Yapısı*, p. 107.

17. Ibid., p. 107.

18. She used the word "pederşahi," which literally translates into patriarchal.

19. The index cited in note 12 was used to compare the prevalence of male authority in the families of the politicians. The averages were as follows: female MPs, 2.3; male MPs, 5.9; and female MC members, 2. In other words, male MPs seemed to feel most acutely the dominance of patriarchal authority.

20. Unlike most people who help with the housework, the person who is with Gaye Akdan is a male. Male help is rare and much more expensive, but considered to be superior to female help. Akdan is concerned about carrying out her household responsibilities well, and can afford to do so.

Chapter 5: Political Involvement: Male Support and Initiation into Politics

1. Ocak was the smallest unit of party organization and was abolished after 1960.

2. The DP leaders pressured the farm laborers not to work for Can's father. The family had to farm its cotton fields itself, as Ece Can puts it, "dropping asleep on the cotton bags out of weariness."

Chapter 6: Getting Elected

1. On career plans of women in the U.S. House of Representatives see Denise Antolini, "The Impact of Women in the U.S. Congress: Ecclesiazusaen Statecraft?" (senior thesis, Princeton University, 1982), p. 21; on routes to political leadership, see Putnam, *Comparative Study of Political Elites*, pp. 45–70.

2. Beyhan Sunar was a lawyer.

3. In rural Anatolia, patron-client networks seem to provide more direct channels that insure candidacy; see Sayarı, *Political Patronage in Turkey* in Gellner and Waterbury, and İlkay Sunar, "Demokrat Parti ve Popülizm" (Democratic Party

and populism) in *Cumhuriyet Dönemi Türkiye Ansiklopedisi* (Encyclopedia of Republican Turkey) 8 (Istanbul: İletişim Yayınları); for a theoretical discussion of channels political elites use to reach the top see Putnam, *Comparative Study of Political Elites*, pp. 45–70.

4. Robert K. Merton, *Social Theory and Social Structure* (New York: Free Press, 1967), p. 424.

5. Identifying the appropriate status sequence to move up the ladder is a problem women generally confront. See Epstein and Coser, *Access to Power*, p. 8.

Chapter 7: Obstacles to Election: Limits to Male Support

1. Kirkpatrick, *Political Women*, Naomi Lynn and Cornelia Butler Flora, "Societal Punishment and Aspects of Female Political Participation: 1972 National Convention Delegates" in Githens and Prestage, *A Portrait of Marginality*, pp. 139–48; also, Melville Currell, *Political Women* (London: Croom Helm Ltd., 1974), pp. 83–90.

2. Mandel, *In The Running*, and "Why Aren't There More Women In Congress" *Congressional Quarterly Weekly Report* (12 August 1978), pp. 2108–2110.

3. Mandel, ibid., pp. 2108–2110.

4. Cynthia Fuchs Epstein, "Women and Power: The Roles of Women in Politics in the United States" in Epstein and Coser, *Access to Power*, pp. 137–38.

5. Lee, *Why Few Women Hold Public Office*; Epstein, *Women and Power*; and Helga Nowotny, "Women in Public Life in Austria" in Epstein and Coser, *Access to Power*, pp. 152–53.

6. A polite form of address for a woman.

7. A polite form of address for a man.

8. The decision as to which candidates are to be nominated rests with the parties alone. It is not the electorate, therefore, but rather the party delegates who choose the male as opposed to the female candidates.

9. See Lloyd and Margaret Fallers, "Sex Roles in Edremit," in J.G. Peristiany, *Mediterranean Family Structures* (Cambridge: Cambridge University Press, 1974), which explains why and how the brother-sister relationship is special in Turkey.

10. "Hanım" and "bey" are forms of address for women and men, respectively, quite common outside politics.

11. "Bizim bey" is the expression she uses to refer to her husband, which literally translates into "our sir."

12. The interrelatedness of the issues they brought up was at times difficult to disentangle. I noted all the different points that came up, regardless of their similarities.

13. See Kirkpatrick, *Political Woman* and Currell, *Political Women*.

14. The primary list.

15. A prominent party leader.

Chapter 8: Conclusion

1. This discussion on women politicians' speeches in the Parliament is summarized from an article by Yeşim Arat, Türkiye'de Kadın Milletvekillerinin Değişen Siyasal Rolleri, 1934–1980" (Changing political roles of women representatives in Turkey) *Journal of Economic and Administrative Sciences* (Bosphorous University,

Winter 1987). See for example Zabıt Ceridesi (ZC) (Parliamentary records) Term 5: 26, p. 26; 25, p. 265, 15 p. 173.

2. ZC Term 5: 12, p. 45; 18, p. 229.
3. ZC Term 9: 7, p. 91.
4. ZC Term 11: 9, p. 618; 12, p. 394.
5. ZC Term 11: 6, p. 160; 2, p. 720; 12, p. 576; 9, p. 618. Also, Term 8: 16, p. 646. And, Term 9: 24, p. 1173, 5, p. 775; 8, p. 264; 8, pp. 162, 163, 211; and 27, p. 269.
6. *Millet Meclisi Tutanakları* (MMT) (Parliamentary records) Term 2: 16, pp. 103–106, 67–69, 436–438, 430–462, 578–579. Also, Term 4: 1, p. 745; 5, p. 153; 3, p. 435.
7. MMT Term 2: 23, pp. 67–68, 330–331; 12, pp. 330–331. Also, Term 5: 14, p. 420; 11, p. 317.
8. *The Situation of Women in the Political Process*, Directorate of Human Rights Council of Europe, 1985 pp. 7–20.
9. For Turkish case studies on this subject see Özbay, "Women's Education in Rural Turkey" in Kâğıtçıbaşı, *Sex Roles, Family and Community in Turkey*, pp. 133–147 and Deniz Kandiyoti, "Rural Transformation in Turkey and its Implications for Women's Stutus," in *Women on the Move* (Paris: United Nations Educational, Scientific, and Cultural Organization, 1984) pp. 17–29.
10. Haavio-Mannila et al., *Unfinished Democracy*, pp. 160–67.

Select Bibliography

Books in English

Abadan-Unat, Nermin, ed. *Women in Turkish Society*. Leiden: E.J. Brill, 1981.

Adıvar, Halide Edip. *Memoirs of Halide Edip Adıvar*. New York: The Century Co., n.d.

Ahmad, Feroz. *The Turkish Experiment in Democracy 1950–1975*. London: Hurst and Co., 1977.

Antolini, Denise. "The Impact of Women in the U.S. Congress: Ecclesiazusaen Statecraft?" Senior thesis, Princeton University, 1982.

Beauvoir, Simone de. *The Second Sex*. New York: Knopf, 1953.

Beck, Lois, and Nikki Keddie. *Women in the Muslim World*. Cambridge: Harvard University Press, 1978.

Bendix, Reinhard. *Max Weber*. Berkeley: University of California Press, 1977.

Berkes, Niyazi. *The Development of Secularism in Turkey*. Montreal: McGill University Press, 1964.

Bernstein, Richard. *Restructuring of Social and Political Theory*. Philadelphia: University of Pennsylvania Press, 1978.

Blood, Robert, and Donald Wolfe. *Husbands and Wives*. New York: Free Press, 1960.

Boulding, Elise, Shirley A. Nuss, Dorothy Lee Carson, and Michael A. Greenstein. *Handbook of International Data on Women*. New York: Halsted Press, John Wiley and Sons, 1976.

Chamberlin, Hope. *A Minority of Members*. New York: Praeger Publishers Inc., 1973.

Chodorow, Nancy. *The Reproduction of Mothering: Psychoanalysis of Gender*. Berkeley, CA: University of California Press, 1978.

Clark, Lorenne M.G., and Lynda Lange, eds. *The Sexism of Social and Political Theory*. Toronto: Toronto University Press, 1979.

Cott, Nancy. *The Bonds of Womanhood: "Woman's Sphere" in New England, 1780–1835*. New Haven: Yale University Press, 1977.

Currell, Melville. *Political Women*. London: Croom Helm Ltd., 1974.

DuBois, Ellen Carol. *Feminism and Suffrage*. Ithaca: Cornell University Press, 1978.

Duverger, Maurice. *The Political Role of Women*. Paris: United Nations Educational, Scientific and Cultural Organisation, 1955.

English, Jane, ed., *Sex Equality*. Englewood Cliffs, N.J.: Prentice Hall Inc., 1977.

Epstein, Cynthia Fuchs, and Rose Laub Coser, eds. *Access to Power: Cross National al Studies of Women and Elites*. London: George Allen and Unwin, 1981.

Eisenstein, Hester and Alice Jardine, eds. *The Future of Difference*. New Brunswick, N.J.: Rutgers University Press, 1985.

Eisenstein, Zillah. *The Radical Future of Liberal Feminism*. New York: Longmans Inc., 1981.

Firestone, Shulamith. *The Dialectic of Sex*. New York: William Morrow and Co., 1970.

Foucoult, Michel. *History of Sexuality*, 1. New York: Pantheon Books, 1978.

Frey, Frederick. *The Turkish Political Elite*. Cambridge: MIT Press, 1965.

Garnett, Lucy. *Turkish Life in Town and Country*. London: George Newness Ltd., 1904.

———. *Women of Turkey and Their Folk-Lore*. London: David Nutt, 1893.

Gellner, Ernest and John Waterbury. *Patrons and Clients in Mediterranean Societies*. London: Duckworth, 1977.

Gibb, H.A.R. et al. *The Encyclopedia of Islam*. Leiden: E.J. Brill, 1960.

Githens, Marianne and Jewel L. Prestage, eds. *A Portrait of Marginality: The Political Behavior of the American Woman*. New York: David Mckay Co., 1977.

Haavio-Mannila, Elina et al., eds. *Unfinished Democracy: Women in Nordic Politics*. Oxford: Pergamon Press, 1985.

Hansen, David. *An Invitation to Critical Sociology: Involvement, Criticism, Exploration*. New York: Free Press, 1976.

Hochschild, Jennifer. *What is Fair?* Cambridge, MA: Harvard University Press, 1981.

Houtsma, M. Th. et al., eds. *The Encyclopedia of Islam*. 3, pt 2. Leiden: E.J. Brill, 1927.

Hyman, H. *Political Socialization*. Glencoe, Ill.: Free Press, 1959.

Issawi, Charles. *The Economic History of Turkey 1800–1914*. Chicago: Chicago University Press, 1980.

Jaquette, Jane, ed. *Women in Politics*. New York: John Wiley and Sons, 1974.

Jenkins, Hester Donaldson. *Behind Turkish Lattices*. London: Collins' Clear Type Press, n.d.

Kâğıtçbaşı, Çiğdem, ed. *Sex Roles, Family and Community in Turkey*. Indiana: Indiana University Turkish Studies, 1982.

Kandiyoti, Deniz, ed. *Major Issues on the Status of Women in Turkey: Approaches and Policies*. Ankara: Çağ Matbaası, 1980.

Keller, Suzanne. *Beyond the Ruling Class: Strategic Elites in Modern Society*. New York: Random House, 1963.

Kelly, Rita Mae and Mary Boutilier. *The Making of Political Woman*. Chicago: Nelson Hall Inc., 1978.

Kinross, Lord. *Atatürk: The Rebirth of a Nation*. London: Unwin Brothers Ltd., 1964.

Kirkpatrick, Jeane. *Political Woman*. New York: Basic Books, 1974.

Klein, Viola. *The Feminine Character*. Chicago: University of Illinois, 1971.

Lamson, Peggy. *Few Are Chosen*. Boston: Houghton Mifflin Co., 1968.

Lane, Robert. *Political Ideology: Why the American Common Man Believes What He Does*. Glencoe, Ill.: Free Press, 1962.

Lenczowski, George, ed. *Political Elites in the Middle East.* Washington, D.C.: AEI Institute, 1975.

Lipset, Seymour Martin. *Political Man.* New York: Doubleday and Co. Inc., 1963.

Levy, Reuben. *The Social Structure of Islam.* Cambridge: Cambridge University Press, 1969.

Lewis, Bernard. *The Emergence of Modern Turkey.* London: Oxford University Press, 1961.

Mandel, Ruth. *In the Running.* New York: Ticknor and Fields, 1981.

Mill, John Stuart. *The Subjection of Women.* Cambridge: MIT Press, 1970.

Montagu, Lady Mary Wortley. *The Complete Letters of Lady Mary Wortley Montagu.* Vol. 1. Edited by Robert Hasband. Oxford: Clarendon Press, 1965.

Mosca, Gaetano, *The Ruling Class.* New York: McGraw Hill, 1939.

Miller, J.B. *Toward a New Psychology of Women.* Boston: Beacon Press, 1976.

Millett, Kate. *Sexual Politics.* New York: Doubleday and Co., 1969.

Nieuwenhuijze, C.A.O. van, ed. *Commoners, Climbers, and Notables.* Leiden: E.J. Brill, 1977.

Penzer, N. *The Harem.* Great Britain: J.B. Lippincott Co., 1936.

Pharr, Susan J. *Political Women in Japan.* Berkeley: University of California Press, 1981.

Putnam, Robert, D. *The Comparative Study of Political Elites.* New Jersey: Prentice Hall, 1976.

Stiehm, Judith, ed. *Women's Views of the Political World of Men.* New York: Transnational Publishers, Inc., 1984.

Tolchin, Susan and Martin Tolchin. *Clout: Womanpower and Politics.* New York: Coward, McCann and Geoghegan Inc., 1973.

United Nations Educational, Scientific and Cultural Organization. *Women On the Move.* Paris: UNESCO, 1984.

U.S. Bureau of the Census. *Statistical Abstract of the United States,* 1979. 100th edition. Washington, D.C.: Government Printing Office, 1979.

U.S. Department of Labor. *Women in the World Today.* International Report I. Washington, D.C.: Government Printing Office, 1963.

Weber, Max. *Economy and Society.* Volume 2. Edited by Guenther Roth and Claus Wittich. Berkeley: University of California Press, 1978.

Weiker, Walter. *Political Tutelage and Democracy in Turkey.* Leiden: E.J. Brill, 1973.

Articles in English

Bem, Sandra. "The Measurement of Psychological Androgyny." *Journal of Consulting and Clinical Psychology* 42, no. 2 (1974): 155–62.

Benston, Margaret. "The Political Economy of Women's Liberation." *Monthly Review* 21, no. 4 (1969): 13–27.

Boals, Kay. "Political Science" (review essay). *Signs: Journal of Women in Culture and Society* 1, no. 1 (Fall 1975): 161–66.

Carroll, Berenice A. "Political Science, Part I: American Politics and Political Behavior." *Signs: Journal of Women in Culture and Society* 5, no. 2 (Winter 1979): 289–306.

Coulson, Margaret, Branka Magas, and Hilary Wainwright. "The Housewife and Her Labor under Capitalism—A Critique." *New Left Review*, no. 89 (January–February 1975): 59–71.

Fox, Greer L. "Another Look at the Comparative Resources Model: Assessing the Balance of Power in Turkish Marriages." *Journal of Marriage and the Family* 35 (November 1973): 718–730.

Frey, Frederik. "Socialization to National Identification Among Turkish Peasants." *Journal of Politics* 30 (November 1968): 934–965.

Gardiner, Jean. "Women's Domestic Labor." *New Left Review*, no. 89 (January–February 1975): 47–58.

Greenstein, Fred. "Socialization: Political Socialization." In *The International Encyclopedia of the Social Sciences*, ed. David Sills, vol. 14, 534–55. New York: Macmillan Co. and Free Press, 1968–1979.

Janeway, Elizabeth. "On the Power of the Weak." *Signs: Journal of Women in Culture and Society* 1, no. 1 (Fall 1975): 103–110.

Katzenstein, Mary Fainsod and David Laitin. "Politics, Feminism and the Ethics of Caring." In *Women and Moral Theory*, ed. Eva Feder Kittay and Diana Meyers. Totowa, N.J.: Rowman and Littlefield, 1987.

Keddie, Nikki. "Problems in the Study of Middle Eastern Women." *International Journal of Middle Eastern Studies* 10, no. 2 (May 1979): 225–240.

Lewis, Bernard. "The Tanzimat and Social Equality." In *Économie et Sociétés dans L'Empire Ottoman*, ed. Jean-Louis Bacqué-Grammont and Paul Dumont, 47. Paris: Editions du Centre National de la Recherche Scientifique, 1983.

Magnarella, Paul. "Aspects of Kinship Change in Modernizing Turkish Towns." *Human Organization* 31, no. 4 (Winter 1972): 361–371.

———. "Conjugal Relationships in a Modernizing Turkish Town." *International Journal of Sociology of the Family* 2, no. 2 (September 1972): 170–181.

Mardin, Şerif. "Religion in Modern Turkey." *International Social Science Journal* 29, no. 2, 1977.

Powell, Lynda Watts. "Male and Female Difference in Elite Political Participation: An Examination of the Effects of Socio Economic and Familial Variables." *The Western Political Quarterly*, March 1981.

Rule, Wilma. "Why Women Don't Run: The Critical Contextual Factors in Women's Legislative Recruitment." *Western Political Quarterly* 34, no. 1, 1981: 73–76.

Safilios-Rothschild, Constantina. "The Study of Family Power Structure: A Review 1960–1969." *Journal of Marriage and the Family* 32, (November 1970): 539–552.

Sayarı, Sabri. "Aspects of Party Organization in Turkey." *Middle East Journal* 30, no. 2 (Spring 1976): 187–199.

Secombe, Wally. "The Housewife and Her Labor under Capitalism." *New Left Review*, no. 83 (January–February 1973): 47–71.

———. "Domestic Labor, a Reply to Critics." *New Left Review*, no. 94 (November–December 1975): 85–96.

Sunar, İlkay, and Binnaz Toprak. "Islam in Politics." *Government and Opposition* 18, no. 4, Autumn 1983.

Watson, Barbara Bellow. "On Power and the Literary Text." *Signs: Journal of Women in Culture and Sciety* 1, no. 1 (Fall 1975): 111–118.

U.S. Congress. "Why Aren't There More Women in Congress." *Congressional Quarterly Weekly Report*, 12 August 1978: 2108–2110.

Books in Turkish

Abadan-Unat, Nermin. *1965 Seçimleri Tahlili* (An analysis of the 1965 elections). Ankara: Sevinç Matbaası, 1967.

Adalet Partisi Kadın Programı (Program of the Justice Party's women's branches). Ankara: n.p., 1963.

Aren, Munise. *Türk Toplumunda Kadın Bibliyografyası* (Women in Turkish society: a bibliography). Ankara: Türk Sosyal Bilimler Derneği, 1980.

Atatürk'ün Söylev ve Demeçleri (Speeches and declarations of Atatürk), vol. 2 (1906–1938). Ankara: Türk Tarih Kurumu Basımevi, 1952.

Corporal, Bernard. *Kemalizmde ve Kemalizm Sonrasında Türk Kadını* (Kemalist and post Kemalist Turkish woman). Ankara: TISA Matbaası, 1982.

Cumhuriyet Halk Partisi Kadın Kolu Programı (Program of the Republican People's Party women's branch). Ankara: n.p., 1969.

Erdem, T., ed. *Seçim Kanunları* (Election laws). Istanbul: Şevket Ünal Matbaası, 1973.

Erişçi, Lütfü. *Türkiye'de İşçi Sınıfı Tarihi* (History of the working class in Turkey). Istanbul: Kutulmuş Basımevi, 1951.

Eyüboğlu, E. Kemal. *Şiirde ve Halk Dilinde Atasözü ve Deyimler* (Proverbs and maxims in poetry and folk language). Istanbul: Doğan Kardeş Matbaacılık Sanayii, 1973.

Inan, Afet. *Tarih Boyunca Türk Kadınının Hak ve Görevleri* (The history of the rights and responsibilities of Turkish women). Istanbul: Milli Eğitim Basımevi, 1975.

———. *Atatürk Hakkında Hatıralar ve Belgeler* (Memoirs and documents on Atatürk). Ankara: Türk Tarih Kurumu Basımevi, 1959.

———. *Atatürk ve Türk Kadın Haklarının Kazanılması* (Atatürk and the emancipation of Turkish women). Istanbul: Milli Eğitim Basımevi, 1968.

Kâğıtçıbaşı, Çiğdem. *Çocuğun Değeri* (Value of children). Istanbul: Boğaziçi Üniversitesi, Gözlem Matbaacılık Koll. Şti., 1981.

Kili, Suna. *CHP'de Gelişmeler* (Developments in the RPP). Istanbul: Çağlayan Basımevi, 1976.

Kıray, Mübeccel. *Ereğli: Ağır Sanayiden önce Bir Sahil Kasabası* (Ereğli: a coastal town before heavy industry). Ankara: TC Başbakanlık Devlet Planlama Teşkilatı, 1964.

Tanpınar, A. Hamdi. *Namık Kemal Antolojisi* (Namık Kemal anthology). Istanbul: Tan Matbassı, 1942.

Taşkıran, Tezer. *Cumhuriyetin 50. Yılında Türk Kadın Hakları* (Turkish women's rights in the fiftieth year of the republic). Ankara: Başbakanlık Basımevi, 1973.

Tekeli, Şirin. *Kadınlar ve Siyasal–Toplumsal Hayat* (Women and sociopolitical life). Istanbul: Yaylacık Matbaası, 1982.

Timur, Serim. *Türkiye'de Aile Yapısı* (Family structure in Turkey). Ankara: Ḥ tepe Üniversitesi Yayını, 1972.

Tokgöz, Oya. *Siyasal Haberleşme ve Kadın* (Political communication and women). Ankara: Sevinç Matbaası, 1979.

158   THE PATRIARCHAL PARADOX

Tunaya, Z.T. *İslamcılık Cereyanı* (The Pan-Islamic Movement). Istanbul: Baha Matbaası, 1962.

Turkey. Büyük Millet Meclisi *Zabıt Ceridesi* (Parliament records). Ankara: Başbakanlık Basımevi, 1935–1960.

Turkey, Büyük Millet Meclisi. Millet Meclisi. *Millet Meclisi Tutanakları* (Congressional records). Ankara: Başbakanlık Basımevi, 1961–80.

Turkey, Millet Meclisi Albümü. *Millet Meclisi Albümü* (Parliamentary albums). Ankara: n.p., 1935–78.

Turkey. Devlet İstatistik Enstitüsü (State Institute of Statistics). *Genel Nüfus Sayımı* (Population census of Turkey), 26 October 1975; 1 percent sample results. Ankara: D.İ.E. Matbaası, 1976.

Turkey. Milli Eğitim Bakanlığı (Turkish Ministry of Education). *Türkiye Cumhuriyeti Milli Eğitim Bakanlığı İlkokul Programı* (Republic of Turkey, ministry of national education elementary school program). Istanbul: Milli Eğitim Basımevi, 1968.

Turkey. Milli Eğitim Bakanlığı. *Türkiye Cumhuriyeti Milli Eğitim Bakanlığı Lise Müfredat Programı* (Republic of Turkey, ministry of national education senior high school program). Ankara: Milli Eğitim Basımevi, 1973.

Turkey. Milli Eğitim Bakanlığı. *Türkiye Cumhuriyeti Milli Eğitim Bakanlığı Ortaokul Programı* (Republic of Turkey, ministry of national education junior high school program). Istanbul: M.E.B. Basımevi, 1970.

Unat, Faik Reşid. *Türkiye'de Eğitim Sisteminin Gelişmesine Tarihi Bir Bakış* (A historical view of the development of the education system). Ankara: Milli Eğitim Basımevi, 1964.

Yücebaş, Hilmi. *Partiler Albümü* (Party albums). Istanbul: Ticaret Matbaası, 1954.

Yücekök, Ahmet. *Türkiye'de Parlamentonun Evrimi* (Evolution of the parliament in Turkey). Ankara: A.Ü.S.B.F. ve Basın Yayın Yüksek Okulu Basımevi, 1983.

Articles in Turkish

Akyol, Mete. "Karı mı Koca mı" (Husband or wife). *Milliyet* 12–18 October 1981.

Gürkan, Ülkü. "Türk Kadınının Hukuki Statüsü ve Sorunları" (Legal status and problems of Turkish women). *Ankara Üniversitesi Hukuk Fakültesi* 35, nos. 1–4.

Kili, Suna. "CHP'de Tüzük Tasarısı ve Gençliğe Yönelik Çelişkiler" (The RPP program draft and its contradictions concerning youth). *Milliyet* 12 November 1976.

Kışlalı, Ahmed Taner. "Siyasal Tutumlarda Kuşak ve Cinsiyet Etkenleri" (Sex and age as determinants of political attitudes). *Ankara Üniversitesi, Siyasal Bilgiler Fakültesi Dergisi* 31, nos. 1–4 (March–April 1976): 116–17.

Tekeli, Şirin. "Kadınların İsteği 'Özgürleşme' mi? 'Eşitlik' mi? Medeni Kanun Tartışmalarının Düşündürdükleri" (Do Women Want "Liberation" or "Equality?" Considerations on the Civil Code Debate). *İktisat Dergisi* (Journal of Economics) (May 1985): 46–50.

―――. "Halk Deyişlerinde Kadın" (Women in folk sayings). *Somut* Haziran, no. 19/20 (1983).

Index

Adıvar, Halide Edip, 26, 28
Aliye, Fatma, 27
Atatürk, Mustafa Kemal, 9, 28–32, 72, 83
Authority: in family, 46, 69, 70, 76, 77, 79; and fathers, 40, 69, 70, 71; and men, 43, 111, 112, 114–19, 121; political, 87, 118; and women, 39, 114; and social roles, 120, 121; structures of, 40, 62, 69, 73–75

Beauvoir, Simone de, 17

Campaign, 66, 67, 90, 101, 105, 119
Candidate(s), 48, 51, 60, 66, 67, 101; Labor Party, 102; at the local level, 64, 95; women, 22, 63, 106, 111, 113, 114–16
Career(s), 95, 96, 98, 105, 107, 124; lines of, 10, 16, 63, 96; patterns of, 72–73; political, 20, 89, 90, 110, 112, 116, 118, 120, 123; professional, 81, 83, 84; and Woman's Branches, 99
Constituencies, 52, 107

Delegates, 48, 64, 101, 102, 110–14, 119, 122
Democratic Party (DP), 48, 51, 52, 88, 89; member of Parliament, 92, 97; rivalry with Republican People's Party, 82, 83, 89, 90, 98, 122; women representatives of, 58, 60
Deputies, 48, 51, 62
Division of labor, 19, 26, 43, 46, 125; and patriarchy, 45, 76–79
Doctors: women, 37, 38, 53

Economic structure, 17, 20
Economy, 17, 18, 36; women's employment in, 74, 117
Education, 27, 39, 40, 72; higher, 53,

54, 119; parliamentarians and, 51, 64; and women, 34–36, 44, 123, 124; women's lack of, 25, 46; and women politicians, 55, 56, 62, 81
Eisenstein, Zillah, 17
Election(s), 22, 47, 104, 116, 118; municipality, 30, 49, 59; to Parliament, 53, 92, 96, 99, 100, 101, 103, 119; to political office, 62, 63, 68, 74, 98, 114; and political parties, 42, 48, 60, 89
Electoral system, 47, 60. *See also* Proportional representation
Electorate, 48, 49; and the candidate, 67, 104, 106, 107, 109, 110, 116
Elgün, Nakiye, 22, 28
Equality, 15, 16, 22, 29, 123

Feminists, 17, 19, 124
Family, 17, 18, 34, 41, 89, 90, 125; equal rights in, 29; income of, 40, 45, 65, 70, 74, 75; and laws, 31; life in, 23, 85; power structure in, 39, 45, 46, 69–71, 79, 118; structure of, 39, 40; and War of Independence, 72
Fathers, 21, 42, 65, 72; and authority, 40, 79, 118, 120; and decision making, 69–71, 76; political inclination of, 85, 86; and women politicians, 86–91, 94, 104, 116, 118, 119
Firestone, Shulamith, 17
Frey, Frederick, 42, 50

Garnett, Lucy, 24, 25
Gender, 81, 107, 119–21, 124, 125; and differences, 16, 17, 20, 35, 36
Gökalp, Ziya, 27, 31

Housewives, 34, 45, 77, 90; and municipality council members, 66, 75, 78, 79
Husband(s), 18, 21, 23, 34, 36, 45, 46, 93; and authority, 40, 73, 74, 76, 118,